Gooseberry Patch

Everyday One-Dish Meals

260

easy, satisfying recipes
for every weeknight!

Oxmoor
House.

Dear Friend,

At the end of a long day, nothing tastes better than a home-cooked meal. But when you have a busy schedule *and* a hungry family to feed, we know it's not always so easy to get dinner on the table. Gooseberry Patch *Everyday One-Dish Meals* is the solution to your need for tasty, fuss-free meals any night of the week. We've created 260 simple, flavor-packed recipes for warming stews and steaming soups, zesty stir fries, cheesy pasta bakes, party-pleasers and more that use ingredients you already have in your pantry.

For easy weeknight meals, try our Honey Chicken Stir-Fry (page 66) or Grilled Salmon BLTs (page 161)…you won't believe just how easy they are to make! For special occasions, our Christmas Eve Pot Roast (page 89) and Feliz Navidad Casserole (page 96) will wow your guests without you having to spend hours in the kitchen. And finally, for a sweet fix, try our scrumptious Berry Easy Cobbler (page 226) or our crowd-pleasing Chocolate-Cappuccino Cheesecake (page 249). You'll also find make-ahead and take-along tips, recipe variations and party-planning ideas throughout the book.

Our well-loved recipes are passed down from generation to generation, shared at potlucks and handed over from neighbors. So whether you're planning a casual week-night meal with family or a fun-filled gathering with friends, Gooseberry Patch *Everyday One-Dish Meals* has you covered. Just remember…cooking a delicious meal doesn't have to be hard!

Happy Cooking!

JoAnn & Vickie
co-founders of Gooseberry Patch

Everyday One-Dish Meals

Pasta with Roasted Veggies,
page 169

contents

Grandma's Baked Mac
& Cheese, page 32

crowd-pleasing delights

If you're searching for that perfect dish for a potluck, Mother's Macaroni Salad is a tried & true dish sure to satisfy partygoers. And favorites like Pizza Roll Snacks and Mother's Fried Chicken will bring smiles to the faces of your guests. Enjoy these and other scrumptious recipes to fit your special occasion.

Scrumptious Stuffed Potato Skins

Scrumptious says it all! Plus, this easy-to-make appetizer will satisfy a hungry crowd. Serve with sour cream, salsa or anything else you like on baked potatoes.

take-along tips

Prepare these potato skins up until the final 20 minutes of baking. Place them on the baking sheet and wrap tightly with foil. Bake them for the final 20 minutes when you arrive at your destination.

4 baking potatoes, quartered
   lengthwise
olive oil
8-oz. container sour cream
⅓ c. shredded Cheddar cheese
1 t. garlic, minced
1 green onion, chopped

2 T. bacon bits
2 t. dried parsley
½ t. salt
½ t. pepper
Garnish: bacon bits, chopped
   green onions, shredded
   Cheddar cheese

Brush potato skins with olive oil; arrange on an ungreased baking sheet cut-side up. Bake at 400 degrees for 30 minutes; cool. Scoop out insides of potatoes, leaving about ⅛-inch shells; reserve scooped-out potato for another use. In a bowl, combine remaining ingredients except garnish and spoon into potato skins; return to baking sheet. Bake an additional 20 minutes. Garnish with additional bacon bits, green onions and Cheddar cheese. Makes 16.

Tammy Rowe
Fremont, OH

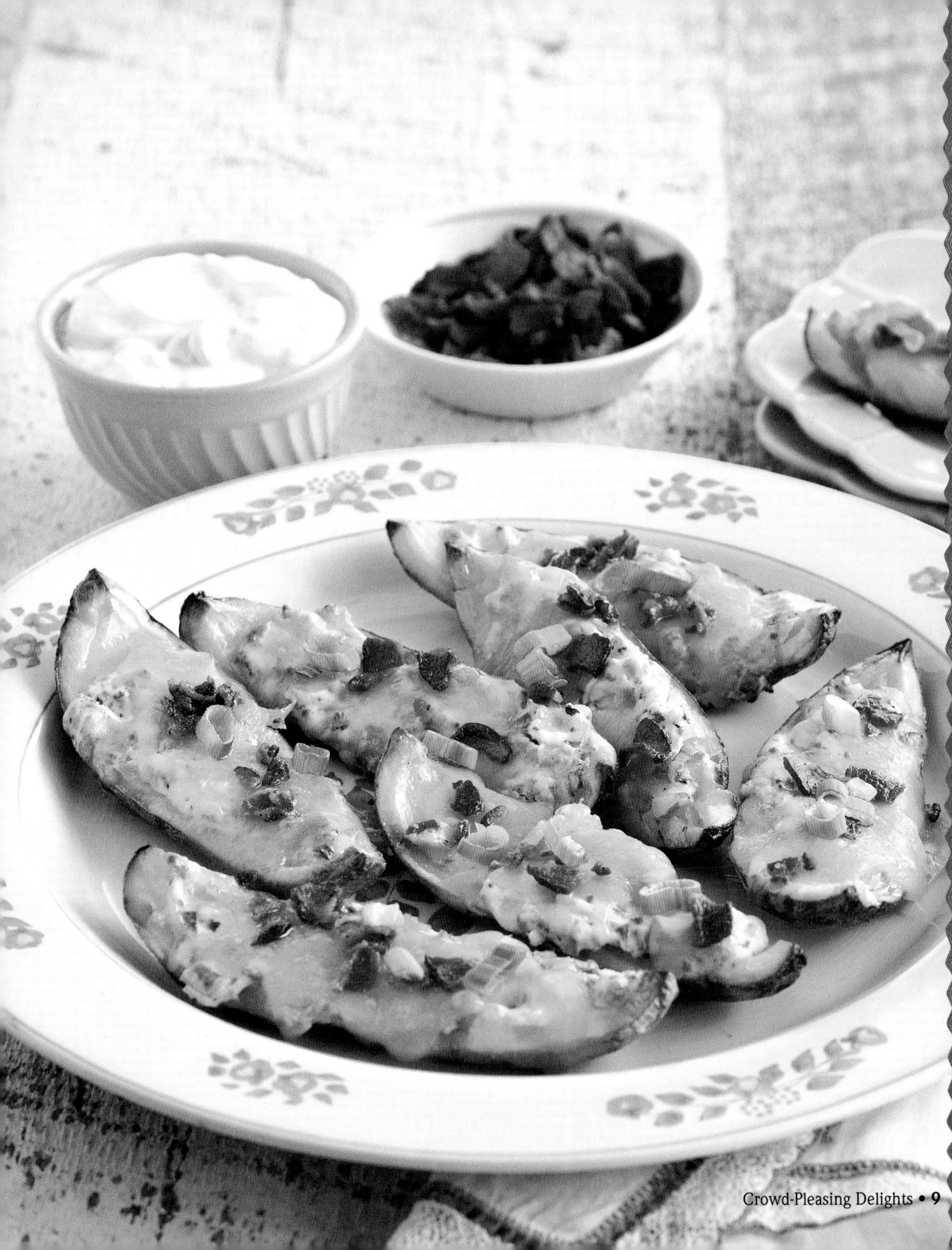

Pizza Roll Snacks

"Who needs frozen pizza rolls when it's a snap to make these yummy rolls? My girls love them for after-school snacks. If there are any leftovers, they warm up great in the microwave."

–Diane

8-oz. tube refrigerated crescent rolls
3 T. pizza sauce
¼ c. grated Parmesan cheese

16 slices pepperoni, divided
⅓ c. shredded mozzarella cheese, divided
Garnish: small fresh basil leaves

Unroll crescent roll dough but do not separate; press perforations to seal. Spread pizza sauce evenly over dough, leaving a one-inch border. Sprinkle with Parmesan cheese and roll up, starting with the long side. Using a sharp knife, cut roll-up into 16 slices. Place slices cut-side down on a greased baking sheet. Top each slice with one pepperoni slice and one teaspoon mozzarella cheese. Bake at 375 degrees for 9 to 11 minutes, until edges are golden and cheese melts. Garnish with basil leaves. Makes 16.

Diane Cohen
The Woodlands, TX

Brown Sugar Fruit Dip

8-oz. pkg. cream cheese,
  softened
½ c. brown sugar, packed
1 c. sour cream
1 t. vanilla extract

1 c. frozen whipped topping,
  thawed
gingersnap cookies and
  assorted fruit slices
Garnish: gingersnap crumbs

In a bowl, beat cream cheese and brown sugar with an electric mixer at medium speed. Add sour cream and vanilla; beat until blended and smooth. Fold in whipped topping. Cover and chill at least 4 hours before serving. Garnish, if desired. Serve with gingersnaps and fruit.
Serves 8 to 10.

Kathy Harris
Valley Center, KS

Hot Ham + Cheddar Dip

1 lb. cooked ham, diced
2 8-oz. pkgs. cream cheese,
  softened
3 c. shredded Cheddar cheese,
  divided

1 onion, diced
1 t. garlic salt
tortilla chips, crackers

In a bowl, blend together all ingredients except chips, reserving ¼ cup Cheddar cheese for topping. Spread ham mixture in a lightly greased 11"x7" baking pan; sprinkle with remaining Cheddar cheese. Bake, uncovered, at 350 degrees for 20 minutes, or until warmed through and cheese is melted. Serve with tortilla chips and crackers. Makes 4 cups.

Jessica Branch
Colchester, IL

take-along tips

Prepare this dish completely except for the baking. Wrap the baking pan tightly with foil to transport it. Complete the baking process when you arrive at your gathering.

mix it up

If you are hosting a party in your home, place a variety of dips with an assortment of vegetables, crackers or chips in different areas of the house so that they won't take up valuable space on your buffet table.

Shredded Beef Sandwiches

12-oz. jar sliced
  pepperoncini
4-lb. beef chuck roast
1¾ t. dried basil
1½ t. dried oregano
1½ t. garlic powder

1¼ t. salt
¼ t. pepper
¼ c. water
1 onion, sliced
10 to 12 sandwich buns, split
  and toasted

"I like to prepare these sandwiches for church get-togethers because they're so tasty."
—Sharon

Pour pepperoncini with liquid into a 5-quart slow cooker; add roast. Mix together spices, salt and pepper in a small bowl; sprinkle over roast. Add water and onion. Cover and cook on low setting for 8 to 9 hours, until meat is tender. Remove roast; shred using 2 forks. Return meat to slow cooker; mix well. Using a slotted spoon, place meat on buns. Serves 10 to 12.

Sharon Beach
Potosi, MO

Old-Fashioned Ham Loaf

> "My mother-in-law, Wilma Scott, is co-chairperson for her church's annual dinner. All of the food they serve is homemade and feeds a crowd of three hundred! This is her recipe."
>
> –Kate

2½ lbs. ground ham
2½ lbs. ground pork
2 c. milk
4 eggs, beaten
2 c. dry bread crumbs

2 c. brown sugar, packed
1 c. vinegar
1 c. water
2 t. mustard

In a large bowl, combine ham and pork; blend well. Add milk, eggs and bread crumbs; mix well. Shape into 20 individual loaves and arrange on lightly greased baking sheets; set aside. Mix together brown sugar, vinegar, water and mustard in a saucepan over medium heat. Heat through and spoon over loaves. Bake at 350 degrees for 1½ to 2 hours. Makes 20 servings.

Kate Scott
Mulberry, IN

Cheesy Ham Strata

12 slices bread, crusts trimmed
¾ lb. Cheddar cheese, sliced
10-oz. pkg. frozen chopped
   broccoli, cooked
2 c. cooked ham, cubed
2 T. dried, minced onion

6 eggs, beaten
3½ c. milk
½ t. salt
¼ t. dry mustard
½ c. shredded Cheddar cheese

Cut out desired shapes from center of each bread slice using cookie cutters; set aside the cut-out shapes and place the remaining bread in a greased 13"x9" baking pan. Layer Cheddar cheese slices over bread pieces; spread broccoli and ham over cheese slices. Sprinkle with onion; arrange cut-out shapes on top. Combine eggs, milk, salt and mustard in a bowl and blend well; pour over top of strata. Cover and refrigerate overnight; bake, uncovered, at 325 degrees for one hour 5 minutes, or until set, sprinkling with shredded Cheddar cheese the last 5 minutes of baking. Let stand 10 minutes before serving. Serves 8.

Vivian Baker
Centerville, OH

Shredded Pork Sandwiches

Roberta Goll (Chesterfield, MI)

Pass the coleslaw. . .perfect with these tender pork sandwiches!

8-lb. pork shoulder roast
1-oz. pkg. onion soup mix
1 c. barbecue sauce

12-oz. can beer or 1½ c. beef broth
40 sandwich buns, split
Garnish: extra barbecue sauce

Combine all ingredients except buns and extra sauce in a 6-quart slow cooker. Cover and cook on low setting for 8 hours. Remove roast from cooking liquid and refrigerate liquid. Using 2 forks, shred roast. Skim fat from surface of cooled liquid. Stir cooking liquid to taste into shredded meat; mix well. Spoon into buns; serve extra sauce on the side. Serves 40.

Company Meatloaf
Phyllis Peters (Three Rivers, MI)

A tried & true recipe that's sure to please!

1 lb. ground pork sausage
3 lbs. ground beef sirloin
1 T. dried sage
8-oz. can tomato sauce
2 c. quick-cooking oats, uncooked

1-oz. pkg. onion soup mix
4 eggs, beaten
2 c. evaporated milk
salt and pepper to taste

Combine all ingredients in a large bowl; mix well. Shape into 2 loaves and place in loaf pans on ungreased baking sheets. Bake at 400 degrees for 30 minutes. Reduce oven temperature to 350 degrees; bake one hour, or until browned. Makes 15 servings.

Papa's Italian Sandwiches

A really tasty sandwich! Keep cooked sausages with sauce mixture separate from rolls and cheese, then assemble the sandwiches when you arrive at your picnic spot.

24 Italian pork sausage links
5 green peppers, thinly sliced
1 onion, chopped
12-oz. can tomato paste
15-oz. can tomato sauce
1 c. water
1 T. sugar
5 cloves garlic, minced
1¼ t. dried oregano
1 t. dried basil
1 t. salt
24 hoagie rolls, split
Garnish: grated Parmesan cheese

Brown 6 to 8 sausages at a time in a large Dutch oven over medium heat. Drain sausages and set aside, reserving 3 tablespoons drippings in Dutch oven. Add peppers and onion. Sauté until crisp-tender; drain. Stir in tomato paste, tomato sauce, water, sugar, garlic, herbs and salt. Add sausages; bring to a boil over medium heat. Reduce heat; simmer, covered, 30 to 45 minutes. Serve on rolls; sprinkle with cheese. Makes 24 servings.

Geneva Rogers
Gillette, WY

picnic perfect

If you're preparing sandwiches before a picnic, slip them into wax paper bags and arrange open-end up in a vintage picnic tin. The bags mean less mess, making sandwiches so much easier for little hands to hold.

Southern-Style Breakfast Casserole

"If I didn't bring this to breakfast on Palm Sunday...I don't think they'd let me in the door!"

–Joyce

2 lbs. ground pork sausage, browned and drained
4 eggs, beaten
½ c. milk
1 onion, diced
6 c. crispy rice cereal
2 c. cooked rice

10¾-oz. can cream of chicken soup
10¾-oz. can cream of celery soup
8-oz. pkg. shredded Cheddar cheese

Combine all ingredients in a large bowl. Pour into a lightly greased 13"x9" baking pan. Bake, uncovered, at 425 degrees for 45 minutes. Serves 8 to 10.

Joyce Boswell
Lewisport, KY

Pork + Apple Meatballs

Serve these yummy meatballs immediately or keep warm in a slow cooker until ready to serve.

1 lb. ground pork sausage
1¼ c. pork-flavored stuffing mix
½ c. low-sodium chicken broth
½ c. Honeycrisp apple, peeled, cored and diced
½ c. onion, diced
1 egg, beaten
1½ t. mustard
½ c. shredded sharp Cheddar cheese
Optional: barbecue sauce

Combine all ingredients except barbecue sauce in a large bowl. Form into balls by tablespoonfuls. Place on a lightly greased 15"x10" jelly-roll pan. Bake at 350 degrees for 18 to 20 minutes, until meatballs are no longer pink in the middle. Brush with barbecue sauce, if desired. Serves 8 to 10.

Emmaline Dunkley
Pine City, MN

avoid a sticky situation

Keep your hands moist with cool water when shaping meatballs to keep them from getting sticky. Use a small ice cream scoop to form the meatballs so they will be the same size and cook evenly.

Mama Ricciuti's Spaghetti Gravy

"My grandfathers and father were born in Italy, and this recipe has been passed down from them."

—Victoria

2 T. olive oil
2-lb. pork shoulder roast
2 lbs. hot ground Italian pork sausage
8 cloves garlic, coarsely chopped
½ c. red wine or beef broth
4 28-oz. cans tomato sauce
3 6-oz. cans tomato paste
4 plum tomatoes, chopped
salt and pepper to taste
2 16-oz. pkgs. spaghetti, cooked
Garnish: grated Parmesan cheese, fresh oregano leaves

Heat oil in a large saucepan over medium heat. Add pork roast, sausage and garlic. Cook until roast and sausage are browned; drain. Add wine or broth; cook one minute and set aside. Combine tomato sauce and tomato paste in a Dutch oven; stir in tomatoes. Add meat mixture, salt and pepper. Simmer over medium heat 2 to 2½ hours. Spoon over hot pasta; garnish with Parmesan cheese and oregano. Serves 10 to 15.

Victoria McElroy
Northbrook, IL

Bishop's Chicken

Note that you'll want to start this recipe one day in advance.

make-ahead magic

Cook the chicken for this dish a day before you plan to serve it. Prepare the remainder of the recipe the following day and serve.

2 3-lb. chickens
1 c. white wine or chicken broth
1 c. water
1½ t. salt
½ t. curry powder
1 onion, sliced
½ c. celery, sliced

2 6-oz. pkgs. long-grain and wild rice, uncooked
2 8-oz. pkgs. sliced mushrooms
¼ c. butter
8-oz. container sour cream
10¾-oz. can golden mushroom soup

Combine chickens and next 6 ingredients in a large stockpot. Bring to a boil over medium-high heat; reduce heat and simmer, uncovered, one hour. Cool. Remove and discard bones and skin; shred meat. Reserve broth and chicken; refrigerate overnight. Next day, skim fat from surface of broth. In a large saucepan, combine rice and reserved broth, adding enough water to cook according to package directions. Stir in chicken and set aside. In a skillet, sauté mushrooms in butter over medium heat; add to chicken mixture. Combine sour cream and soup in a bowl; stir into chicken mixture. Spoon into a greased 13"x9" baking pan. Bake, uncovered, at 350 degrees for one hour. Serves 8 to 10.

Doris Zinck
Lincoln University, PA

Kay's Chinese Chicken Salad

3-oz. pkg. chicken ramen
  noodles with seasoning
  packet, uncooked
1 head cabbage, shredded
4 boneless, skinless chicken
  breasts, cooked and shredded

2 T. red onion, chopped
2 T. sliced almonds, toasted
2 T. sesame seeds, toasted

"Last year I hosted a ladies' potluck luncheon, and my good friend Kay brought this salad. Everyone thought it was marvelous!"

–Linda

Set aside ramen noodle seasoning packet for dressing; crush noodles. Combine all ingredients except seasoning packet in a large serving bowl; toss lightly to combine. Drizzle with Dressing and toss again. Serves 8 to 10.

Dressing:

1 c. vegetable oil
3 T. sugar
⅓ c. vinegar
2 t. salt

1 t. pepper
reserved ramen noodle
  seasoning packet

Whisk together all ingredients in a bowl. Makes 1 cup.

Linda Galvin
Ames, IA

Old-Fashioned
Chicken Pot Pie

Old-Fashioned Chicken Pot Pie

This makes two savory pies. . .share one with a neighbor or freeze it to enjoy later. For convenience, use refrigerated pie crusts instead of frozen. Look for them near prepared cookie dough and biscuits at the grocery store.

4 9-inch frozen pie crusts, thawed and divided
5 to 6 boneless, skinless chicken breasts, cooked and chopped
1 onion, chopped
10¾-oz. can cream of chicken soup
10¾-oz. can cream of mushroom soup
8-oz. container sour cream
salt and pepper to taste

Line two 9" pie plates with one crust each; set aside. Combine chicken, onion, soups, sour cream and salt and pepper to taste in a large bowl; mix well. Divide between bottom pie crusts; top with remaining crusts. Crimp crusts to seal and cut several slits in top. Bake at 350 degrees for 35 to 45 minutes, until filling is bubbly and crusts are golden. Makes 2 pies, 6 servings each.

Donna Riggins
Albertville, AL

Mother's Fried Chicken

4 c. self-rising flour
2 T. salt
2 T. coarse pepper
8 lbs. chicken
4 to 5 c. shortening, divided

Combine flour, salt and pepper in a shallow pan. Dredge chicken in flour mixture. In a large cast-iron skillet over medium-high heat, heat 3 cups shortening to 350 degrees. Working in batches, fry chicken, covered, about 10 minutes. Reduce heat to medium-low; fry 30 minutes per side. Add shortening as needed. Uncover during last 5 minutes of cooking time. Drain on paper towels. Serves 8.

Evelyn Russell
Dallas, TX

"This recipe was given to me by my mother 30 years ago. It is almost always asked for when I cook for church get-togethers and Sunday dinners."

—Evelyn

The Best-Yet Buffalo Wings

These wings are sweet, but the sauce is hot!

3 lbs. chicken wings
seasoned salt to taste
2-oz. bottle hot pepper sauce

1 c. brown sugar, packed
1 c. water
1 T. mustard seed

Arrange chicken wings on a lightly greased 15"x10" jelly-roll pan. Sprinkle with seasoned salt. Bake at 400 degrees for 20 minutes; turn wings. Bake 20 to 30 more minutes, until golden and juices run clear when chicken is pierced with a fork; drain. Arrange on serving platter. Combine remaining ingredients in a saucepan; bring to a boil over medium heat. Reduce heat to low; cook until mixture caramelizes and becomes a dark burgundy color, stirring occasionally. Pour sauce over wings before serving, or serve on the side for dipping. Makes about 3 dozen.

Kristen Taylor
Fort Smith, AR

clean hands

A tray of warm, moistened towels is a must when serving sticky barbecue ribs or chicken wings! Dampen fingertip towels in water and a dash of lemon juice, roll up and microwave on high 10 to 15 seconds.

Church Bazaar Chicken à la King

Not only is this absolutely delicious, it's oh-so perfect when you're looking for a recipe that's just right for a large get-together!

3 c. butter
3½ c. all-purpose flour
salt to taste
9 c. milk, warmed
6 lbs. cooked chicken, diced

2 4-oz. jars diced pimentos, drained
2 8-oz. pkgs. mushrooms, chopped
cooked rice or noodles

Melt butter in a large saucepan over medium heat; remove from heat. Stir in flour, a little at a time, whisking until smooth. Sprinkle with salt; gradually add warmed milk, whisking constantly. Bring to a boil, stirring until smooth and thick, about 15 to 20 minutes. Stir in chicken, pimentos and mushrooms; simmer until heated through. Serve with rice or noodles. Serves 50.

Wendy Jacobs
Idaho Falls, ID

take-along tips

Prepare the dish completely and transport it in a large plastic container with a lid. Take along a second large container filled with prepared rice or noodles. Either serve straight from these containers or take along pretty dishes for serving.

Almond Tea Sandwiches

Serve these triangle-shaped sandwiches stacked on a tiered stand.

¾ c. butter, softened
½ c. fresh basil, chopped
2 t. lemon juice
⅛ t. salt
20 slices favorite bread

1 c. cooked chicken, finely chopped
½ c. mayonnaise
½ c. slivered almonds
salt and pepper to taste

Combine butter, basil, lemon juice and salt in a bowl. Spread each slice of bread with a thin layer of butter mixture. Combine remaining ingredients in a separate bowl; spread on half the bread slices. Top with remaining bread slices butter-side down. Remove crusts; slice into triangles. Makes 40.

Michelle Sheridan
Huntsville, AL

Creamy Turkey Lasagna

make-ahead magic

Use leftover turkey from family holiday feasts to make this delicious casserole.

10¾-oz. can cream of mushroom soup
10¾-oz. can cream of chicken soup
1 c. grated Parmesan cheese
1 c. sour cream
¼ c. chopped pimentos
2 to 3 c. cooked turkey, chopped

1 c. onion, chopped
½ t. garlic salt
8-oz. pkg. lasagna noodles, cooked
2 c. shredded Cheddar cheese
Garnish: chopped fresh parsley

Combine soups, Parmesan cheese, sour cream, pimentos, turkey, onion and garlic salt in a large bowl; mix well. Spread one-fourth of turkey mixture on the bottom of a lightly greased 13"x9" baking pan; place noodles on top. Alternate layers of remaining turkey mixture and noodles; top with Cheddar cheese. Bake, uncovered, at 350 degrees for 40 to 45 minutes. Let stand 10 minutes before serving. Garnish with parsley. Serves 8.

Jennifer Eveland
Blandon, PA

Church Supper Tuna Bake

An old-fashioned favorite that everyone loves.

¼ c. butter
¾ c. green pepper, diced
3 c. celery, sliced
2 onions, chopped
3 10¾-oz. cans cream of
  mushroom soup
2 c. milk
12-oz. pkg. American cheese,
  cubed

24-oz. pkg. medium egg
  noodles, cooked
1½ c. mayonnaise
4-oz. jar chopped pimentos,
  drained
3 9½-oz. cans tuna, drained
1 c. slivered almonds, toasted

Melt butter in a skillet over medium heat. Add pepper, celery and onions; sauté 10 minutes, or until tender. Combine soup and milk in a large stockpot; add vegetable mixture and heat through. Stir in cheese until melted. In a large bowl, mix together cooked noodles and 2 cups soup mixture; toss to coat. Spread in 2 lightly greased 13"x9" baking pans. Stir mayonnaise, pimentos and tuna into remaining soup mixture. Pour over noodles and mix gently; sprinkle with almonds. Bake, uncovered, at 375 degrees for 35 to 40 minutes. Serves 25.

Stephanie Mayer
Portsmouth, VA

time-saver

Save time by cooking a casserole ahead…it's easy! Line the casserole dish with aluminum foil, leaving a 2-inch overhang around edges. Add casserole ingredients, bake as directed, cool and freeze, uncovered. When it is completely frozen, lift the casserole out using the aluminum foil overhang. Cover and freeze. To thaw, simply place the casserole in the dish it was originally baked in.

Garden-Fresh Zucchini Quiche

4 c. zucchini, grated
1½ c. biscuit baking mix
½ c. vegetable oil
3 eggs, beaten
1 t. dried oregano
½ t. salt
½ t. pepper
1½ c. shredded Cheddar
   cheese
½ c. onion, chopped

In a large bowl, mix together zucchini, baking mix, oil and eggs until well blended. Add remaining ingredients. Pour into a lightly greased 9" deep-dish pie plate. Bake at 400 degrees for 25 minutes. Serves 8.

Lori Ritchey
Denver, PA

Cheesy Spinach Pie

Two cheeses combine to make this dish delectable.

2 c. cottage cheese
⅔ c. feta cheese, crumbled
¼ t. pepper
10-oz. pkg. frozen chopped
   spinach, thawed and drained
3 eggs
¼ c. butter, melted
2 T. all-purpose flour
2 t. dried, minced onion

In a large bowl, combine ingredients in order listed; mix well. Spread in a greased 1½-quart casserole dish. Bake, uncovered, at 350 degrees for 45 minutes, or until center is set. Serves 8.

Janine Kuras
Warren, MI

Louisiana Shrimp Boil

Just for fun, serve this meal with sliced French bread on a picnic table outdoors…and be sure to pass plenty of paper towels!

4 onions, sliced
4 lemons, sliced
2 3-oz. pkgs. crab boil
   seasoning
Optional: hot pepper sauce to
   taste

32 new redskin potatoes
8 ears corn, husked and halved
4 lbs. uncooked medium
   shrimp in the shell

Fill a very large stockpot half full with water; add onions, lemons, seasoning and hot pepper sauce, if using. Bring water to a boil over medium-high heat; add potatoes and boil 10 minutes. Add corn; boil 5 minutes. Add shrimp; boil until shrimp turn pink and float to the surface. Drain; serve on a large platter. Serves 8.

Janet Bowlin
Fayetteville, AR

Grandma's Baked Mac & Cheese

"My grandma is famous at her church for this recipe and is always asked to bring it for church suppers or luncheons."

—Rebecca

2 16-oz. pkgs. jumbo elbow
  macaroni, uncooked
1½ c. butter, divided
1 to 1½ c. all-purpose flour
4 to 6 c. milk

1½ lbs. pasteurized process
  cheese spread, cubed
16-oz. pkg. shredded sharp
  Cheddar cheese
1½ c. dry bread crumbs

Prepare macaroni according to package directions. Pour macaroni into a very large bowl; set aside. Melt ¾ cup butter in a saucepan over medium heat; whisk in one cup flour. If sauce is thin, add more flour. Add 4 cups milk; whisk to blend well. If needed, add more milk. Stir in cheese spread until melted. Add shredded cheese; mix until melted. Pour sauce over macaroni; mix well. Spread mixture in a lightly greased 15"x12" baking pan or smaller baking pans. Melt remaining butter in a saucepan. Stir in bread crumbs; mix until butter is absorbed. Sprinkle over macaroni. Bake, uncovered, at 350 degrees for about 30 minutes, until golden and bubbly. Serves 25 to 30.

Rebecca LaMere
Yulee, FL

Mother's Macaroni Salad

A tried & true recipe with old-fashioned flavor.

8 eggs, divided
1 c. cider vinegar
1 c. water
2½ c. sugar
2 T. all-purpose flour
1 T. dry mustard
1 t. salt

½ t. celery seed
⅛ t. ground ginger
2 c. mayonnaise
2 16-oz. pkgs. elbow
   macaroni, cooked
⅓ c. onion, finely chopped
2 stalks celery, chopped

Hard-boil, peel and finely chop 4 eggs; set aside. Beat remaining 4 eggs in a small bowl. In a saucepan over low heat, combine vinegar, water, sugar, flour, mustard, salt, celery seed, ginger and beaten eggs. Cook and stir until boiling. Remove from heat and let cool; stir in mayonnaise. Combine cooked macaroni, hard-boiled eggs, onion and celery in a large bowl; pour vinegar mixture over all. Stir well; chill until serving time. Makes 14 to 16 servings.

Kate Haney
Ellensburg, WA

Fried Okra Salad
Lisa Martin (Tulsa, OK)

"I took this dish to a ladies' function at my church, and by the time it was over, everyone had copied the recipe!" –Lisa

24-oz. pkg. frozen breaded okra
10 slices bacon, crisply cooked
   and crumbled
6 roma tomatoes, chopped

1 bunch green onions, chopped
½ c. olive oil
¼ c. sugar
2 T. vinegar

Fry okra according to package directions; drain. Combine okra, bacon, tomatoes and green onions in a large bowl; set aside. Mix together remaining ingredients in a small bowl; pour over okra mixture. Best served at room temperature. Serves 8.

Best-Ever Tortellini Salad

"This is an excellent salad to take to church socials."

2 9-oz. pkgs. cheese tortellini, cooked
2 red or green peppers, chopped
1 red onion, chopped
3.8-oz. can sliced black olives, drained
½ c. white vinegar
½ c. olive oil
3 T. fresh mint, chopped
2 T. cooking sherry or orange juice
1 T. lemon juice
1½ t. garlic powder
¼ t. red pepper flakes
4-oz. pkg. crumbled feta cheese

Combine tortellini, peppers, onion and olives in a large serving bowl; set aside. Combine remaining ingredients except feta cheese in a small bowl; pour over tortellini mixture. Chill 4 to 24 hours before serving. Sprinkle with feta cheese. Serves 8.

Priscilla Reed
Rindge, NH

Southwestern Layered Salad

15-oz. can black beans, drained and rinsed
¼ c. salsa
2 c. lettuce, chopped
2 tomatoes, chopped
15¼-oz. can corn, drained
1 green pepper, chopped
1 red onion, finely chopped
½ c. shredded Cheddar cheese
¼ c. bacon bits
Italian salad dressing to taste

Combine black beans and salsa in a small bowl. In a large trifle bowl, layer bean mixture, lettuce, tomatoes, corn, green pepper, onion and cheese. Sprinkle with bacon bits; drizzle with dressing. Refrigerate until ready to serve. Serves 8.

Lori Downing
Bradenton, FL

Potluck Pasta Salad

Try this salad with veggies like yellow squash or peas.

12-oz. pkg. rainbow rotini pasta, uncooked
16-oz. bottle zesty Italian salad dressing
1 t. red pepper flakes
2¼-oz. can sliced black olives, drained
1 cup sliced green olives, drained

4 oz. smoked Cheddar cheese, cubed
4 oz. Pepper Jack cheese, cubed
4 oz. pepperoni, cubed
4 oz. salami, cubed
½ c. green onions, sliced
6-oz. can smoked almonds

Cook pasta according to package directions; drain and rinse with cold water. Place in a large salad bowl; cool to room temperature. Stir in all ingredients except almonds; cover and refrigerate at least 2 hours. Stir in almonds at serving time. Makes 6 to 8 servings.

Joy Diomede
Double Oak, TX

Mamma Mia Italian Stew

This slow-cooker stew is chock-full of flavorful summer produce, with a hint of heat from hot Italian sausage.

1 lb. hot ground Italian sausage, cooked and drained
1 eggplant, peeled and cubed
1½ c. sliced green beans
2 green peppers, sliced
1 to 2 potatoes, peeled and cubed
1 large zucchini, cubed
1 large yellow squash, cubed
1 c. onion, thinly sliced
15-oz. can Italian-style tomato sauce
¼ c. olive oil
2 t. garlic, minced
1 t. salt

Combine all ingredients in a 7-quart slow cooker; stir well. Cover and cook on low setting for 8 hours or on high setting for 4 hours. Serves 8 to 10.

Connie Bryant
Topeka, KS

seasonal menus

Thinking of a menu for guests? Let the season be your guide! Soups and stews brimming with the harvest's bounty are just right for fall get-togethers, and juicy fruit salads are delightful in the summer. Not only will you get the freshest ingredients when you plan by the season, but you'll also get the best prices at the supermarket!

Black-Eyed Pea Soup

6 slices bacon
1 onion, finely chopped
1 clove garlic, minced
½ t. salt
½ t. pepper
4-oz. can chopped green chiles, drained
4 15½-oz. cans black-eyed peas, undrained
2 14½-oz. cans beef broth
10-oz. can diced tomatoes with green chiles
cornbread

Cook bacon in a Dutch oven until crisp; remove bacon, reserving drippings in pan. Crumble bacon and set aside. Add onion, garlic, salt, pepper and chiles to bacon drippings; sauté over medium heat until onion is golden. Add bacon, peas, broth and tomatoes with green chiles. Increase heat to medium-high and bring to a boil; remove from heat. Serve with cornbread. Serves 12 to 14.

Old-Fashioned Veggie Soup

4 c. beef broth
1¾ c. potatoes, peeled and diced
1½ c. onion, chopped
1 c. carrots, sliced
1 c. celery, sliced
½ t. dried basil
½ t. pepper
¼ t. salt
¼ t. dried thyme
2 bay leaves
2 28-oz. cans whole tomatoes, undrained
10-oz. pkg. frozen corn, partially thawed
10-oz. pkg. frozen baby lima beans, partially thawed
10-oz. pkg. frozen sliced okra, partially thawed
pepper to taste

Combine first 10 ingredients in a large stockpot. Purée tomatoes in a blender; add to stockpot. Bring to a boil; reduce heat and simmer, covered, 40 minutes. Add corn and lima beans; simmer until tender, stirring occasionally. Add okra and bring to a boil; reduce heat and simmer 5 minutes. Add pepper to taste. Discard bay leaves before serving. Serves 8.

Amy Biermann
Riverside, OH

Old-Fashioned
Veggie Soup

Chicken-Pepper
Pasta, page 61

memorable main dishes

When it's dinnertime, you need hearty, homestyle meals that come together in a hurry. Try family favorites such as Zesty Pizza Casserole, Spicy Taco Salad, and Apple-Stuffed Pork Chops. The simple recipes found throughout these pages provide comfort for a busy lifestyle.

One-Pot Spaghetti

1 lb. ground beef
1 onion, diced
2 14-oz. cans chicken broth
6-oz. can tomato paste
½ t. dried oregano
½ t. salt
¼ t. pepper
⅛ t. garlic powder
8-oz. pkg. spaghetti, uncooked
  and broken
Garnish: grated Parmesan
  cheese

Brown ground beef and onion in a large skillet over medium heat. Drain; return to skillet. Stir in broth, tomato paste and seasonings; bring to a boil. Add spaghetti; reduce heat and simmer, stirring often, 15 minutes, or until spaghetti is tender. Sprinkle with cheese. Makes 4 servings.

Flo Burtnett
Gage, OK

Southwestern Casserole

The kids will love this…and the grown-ups too!

2 lbs. ground beef
1 onion, chopped
2 10-oz. cans enchilada sauce
2 16-oz. cans chili beans with
  sauce
13½-oz. pkg. tortilla chips,
  divided
8-oz. pkg. shredded Cheddar
  cheese
Garnish: sour cream, chopped
  fresh cilantro

Brown ground beef and onion in a skillet over medium heat; drain. Stir in enchilada sauce and beans. Coarsely break up tortilla chips, reserving ½ cup. Arrange remaining chips in a lightly greased 13"x9" baking pan; spread beef mixture on top. Sprinkle with reserved ½ cup tortilla chips and Cheddar cheese. Cover and bake at 350 degrees for 30 minutes. Serve immediately, garnished with sour cream and cilantro. Serves 6.

Bobbi Carney
Arvada, CO

Southwestern
Casserole

Zesty Pizza Casserole

Add your favorite pizza toppings to this easy casserole.

make-ahead magic

You can prepare this tasty casserole a day in advance and store it overnight in the refrigerator.

1 lb. ground beef
½ c. onion, chopped
½ c. green pepper, chopped
2 16-oz. cans pizza sauce
4-oz. can mushrooms, drained
4-oz. pkg. sliced pepperoni
½ t. salt
½ t. dried oregano
½ t. garlic powder
½ t. dried basil
2 c. cooked elbow macaroni
¾ c. shredded mozzarella cheese
Garnish: sliced fresh basil

Brown ground beef with onion and green pepper in a large skillet over medium heat; add remaining ingredients except mozzarella cheese and garnish. Pour into a lightly greased 2-quart casserole dish; sprinkle with cheese. Bake, uncovered, at 350 degrees for 30 to 45 minutes. Garnish with basil. Serves 4 to 6.

Valerie Neeley
Robinson, IL

Cream Cheese Enchiladas

2 8-oz. pkgs. cream cheese,
  softened
1 c. sour cream
2 10-oz. cans mild green chile
  enchilada sauce
¼ c. jalapeño peppers, seeded
  and chopped
1 lb. ground beef, browned and
  drained

½ c. shredded sharp Cheddar
  cheese
8 to 12 flour tortillas
1 sweet onion, chopped
½ c. sliced black olives
Garnish: sliced black olives,
  chopped tomato, shredded
  lettuce, chopped green
  onions, salsa, shredded
  cheese

"This creamy variation on Mexican enchiladas is yummy! It won me first place in a local newspaper's holiday cooking contest."

—Mary Kathryn

In a large bowl, blend together cream cheese, sour cream, enchilada sauce and jalapeños; set aside. Combine ground beef and shredded cheese in another bowl; set aside. Fill each tortilla with one to 2 tablespoons cream cheese mixture and one to 2 tablespoons beef. Sprinkle each with onion and olives; roll up tortillas. Place seam-side down in an ungreased 13"x9" baking pan; cover with remaining cream cheese mixture. Bake, uncovered, at 400 degrees for 30 to 40 minutes; cover if top begins to brown. Garnish as desired. Makes 8 servings.

Mary Kathryn Carter
Platte City, MO

Chili-Beef Enchiladas

½ lb. ground beef
10¾-oz. can chili-beef soup,
   divided
¼ c. catsup
2 T. onion, chopped
½ t. garlic powder

¼ t. chili powder
⅛ t. ground cumin
8 corn tortillas
½ c. shredded Cheddar
   cheese, divided
½ c. water

Combine ground beef, ¼ cup soup, catsup, onion and spices in a one-quart glass measuring cup. Microwave, uncovered, on high 5 minutes, stirring once to separate beef; set aside. Wrap 2 tortillas in a damp paper towel; microwave on high 40 seconds. Immediately spoon beef mixture onto both tortillas; top each with one tablespoon cheese. Roll up tightly; place seam-side down in an ungreased 1½-quart shallow glass dish. Repeat until all tortillas are filled. In a small bowl, mix remaining soup and water; pour over enchiladas. Microwave, uncovered, on high 10 to 12 minutes, until hot, turning dish one-half turn every 4 minutes. Serves 4.

April Jacobs
Loveland, CO

Salsa Ranch Skillet

1 lb. ground beef
½ c. sweet onion, chopped
½ c. green pepper, chopped
1-oz. pkg. ranch salad dressing
   mix
1 c. water
15-oz. can tomato sauce

16-oz. jar mild salsa
16-oz. can baked beans
8-oz. pkg. rotini pasta,
   uncooked
1 c. shredded Colby Jack
   cheese

Brown ground beef with onion and green pepper in a large skillet over high heat. Stir in dressing mix until blended. Stir in water, tomato sauce, salsa and beans; bring to a boil. Add pasta; reduce heat to medium-low. Simmer 12 to 15 minutes, until pasta is tender, stirring occasionally. Remove from heat; sprinkle with cheese and let stand 5 minutes. Serves 4 to 6.

Mandi Smith
Delaware, OH

Spicy Taco Salad

For a party presentation, place tortilla chips on a platter and top with ground beef and vegetables arranged in rings. Spoon the avocado sauce over all.

1 lb. ground beef
1 head lettuce, shredded
15½-oz. can kidney beans,
  drained and rinsed
3 tomatoes, chopped
4 green onions, chopped
1 c. shredded Monterey Jack
  cheese
2 avocados, diced

¼ c. vegetable oil
1 c. sour cream
1 T. sugar
1 T. chili powder
2 T. lemon juice
salt to taste
⅛ t. hot pepper sauce
10-oz. pkg. tortilla chips

take-along tips

Prepare this recipe and put it in a portable container. Simply transfer it to a platter when ready to serve.

Brown ground beef in a skillet over medium heat; drain and let cool. In a large bowl, toss together beef, lettuce, beans, tomatoes, green onions, cheese and avocados; set aside. In a small bowl, combine remaining ingredients except tortilla chips. Layer chips and beef mixture. Top with dressing. Serves 4.

Allene Whalen
Salinas, CA

Family-Favorite Chili Mac

Stephanie McNealy (Talala, OK)

Kids love this quick & easy dinner. Serve with a tossed salad and cornbread sticks.

2 7¼-oz. pkgs. macaroni & cheese, uncooked
10-oz. can diced tomatoes with green chiles
1 to 2 lbs. ground beef
1¼-oz. pkg. taco seasoning mix
chili powder to taste
salt and pepper to taste

Prepare macaroni & cheese according to package directions. Stir in tomatoes with green chiles; set aside. Brown ground beef in a skillet over medium-high heat; drain and mix in taco seasoning. Stir beef mixture into macaroni mixture. Add seasonings as desired; heat through. Serves 8.

Steak & Mushrooms Packets

The steak strips will be much easier to cut if you freeze the meat for about 15 minutes first.

1 lb. boneless round steak,
  cut into thin strips
½ t. garlic powder
½ t. pepper

12-oz. pkg. sliced mushrooms
½ c. teriyaki sauce
½ c. green onions, sliced
cooked rice or noodles

Sprinkle steak strips with garlic powder and pepper; place in a large plastic zipping bag. Add mushrooms and teriyaki sauce; mix well. Seal and refrigerate 2 to 4 hours. Divide steak mixture among 4 squares of aluminum foil; top with green onions. Bring up aluminum foil around ingredients; seal packets tightly. Place on a baking sheet; bake at 350 degrees for 12 to 15 minutes. Serve over cooked rice or noodles. Serves 4.

Melanie Lowe
Dover, DE

Chili-Rubbed Steaks

Rubs are a great, quick way to give steaks delicious flavor.

1 T. ground cumin
2 t. chili powder
½ t. salt

⅛ t. pepper
3 boneless sirloin steaks,
   about ½-inch thick

In a small bowl, mix together seasonings and rub on both sides of steaks; let stand 5 to 10 minutes. Lightly oil grill rack; place steaks on grill. Cover and cook over medium heat 3 to 5 minutes per side for medium-rare. Slice each steak in half; mound each with a generous portion of Chunky Guacamole Salsa. Serve any remaining guacamole on the side. Serves 6.

Chunky Guacamole Salsa:

2 avocados, diced
2 plum tomatoes, chopped
1 jalapeño pepper, chopped
2 T. lime juice
2 T. shallots, chopped

2 T. fresh cilantro, chopped
1½ t. ground cumin
½ t. salt
2 T. vegetable oil

Place avocados, tomatoes and jalapeño pepper in a medium bowl; set aside. In a small bowl, mix together lime juice, shallots, cilantro, cumin and salt; whisk in oil. Pour over avocado mixture; mix well. Serves 6.

Beverly Ray
Brandon, FL

Pepper Steak Sammies

1 to 1¼ lbs. beef sirloin or
   ribeye steak
2 green peppers, thinly sliced
1 onion, sliced
4 cloves garlic, minced and
   divided

1 T. vegetable oil
salt and pepper to taste
⅓ c. butter, softened
4 French rolls, split and
   toasted

Grill or broil steak to desired doneness; set aside. Sauté green peppers, onion and 2 cloves garlic in hot oil in a skillet over medium heat until crisp-tender; drain. Slice steak thinly; add to skillet and heat through. Sprinkle with salt and pepper. Blend butter and remaining garlic in a small bowl; spread over cut sides of rolls. Spoon steak mixture onto bottom halves of rolls; cover with tops. Makes 4 sandwiches.

Vickie
Gooseberry Patch

take-along tips

Grill the meat and sauté vegetables in advance and wrap them in aluminum foil. When you arrive at your destination, assemble the meat and veggies on French rolls and serve.

Swiss Bliss

"I've had this recipe over 30 years. It's great with mashed potatoes."

—Brenda

2 lbs. beef chuck roast, cut
　into 4 to 6 pieces
1½-oz. pkg. onion soup mix
16-oz. can diced tomatoes,
　drained and ½ c. juice
　reserved
8-oz. pkg. sliced mushrooms

½ green pepper, sliced
¼ t. salt
pepper to taste
1 T. steak sauce
1 T. cornstarch
1 T. fresh parsley, chopped

Arrange beef pieces, slightly overlapping, on a greased 20-inch length of aluminum foil. Sprinkle with onion soup mix; top with tomatoes, mushrooms, green pepper, salt and pepper. Mix together reserved tomato juice, steak sauce and cornstarch in a small bowl; pour over meat and vegetables. Bring up aluminum foil around ingredients and double-fold edges to seal tightly. Place foil package in a baking pan. Bake at 375 degrees for 2 hours, or until tender. Sprinkle with parsley. Serves 4 to 6.

Brenda Doak
Delaware, OH

Orange-Pork Stir-Fry

Short on time? Pick up a package of pork that's precut into strips for stir-frying.

1-oz. pkg. Italian salad
　dressing mix
¼ c. orange juice
¼ c. vegetable oil
2 T. soy sauce

1 lb. pork loin, cut into strips
14-oz. pkg. frozen Oriental
　vegetable blend, thawed
2½ c. cooked rice

In a small bowl, mix together dressing mix, juice, oil and soy sauce. Combine one tablespoon of dressing mixture and pork strips in a large skillet over medium heat. Cook, stirring constantly, 4 to 5 minutes, until pork is no longer pink. Add vegetables and remaining dressing mixture; cook 6 minutes, stirring frequently, until vegetables are crisp-tender. Serve over cooked rice. Makes 4 servings.

Amy Butcher
Columbus, GA

Apple-Stuffed Pork Chops

A scrumptious way to serve pork chops. So easy to make, but it looks like you spent hours in the kitchen!

6 thick pork chops
salt and pepper to taste
1½ c. toasted bread crumbs
½ c. apple, cored and chopped
½ c. shredded sharp Cheddar cheese

2 T. raisins
2 T. butter, melted
2 T. orange juice
¼ t. salt
⅛ t. cinnamon

Cut a pocket into the side of each pork chop; sprinkle pockets with salt and pepper. Set aside. In a medium bowl, toss together bread crumbs, apple, cheese and raisins; set aside. In a small bowl, combine butter, orange juice, salt and cinnamon; stir into apple mixture. Stuff pockets with mixture; place in an ungreased 13"x9" baking pan. Bake, uncovered, at 350 degrees for 15 minutes. Cover and bake an additional 15 minutes. Makes 6 servings.

Chuck Wagon Chops

Substitute sweet potatoes for a different taste…use your favorite spicy flavor of barbecue sauce too!

6 bone-in pork chops
salt and pepper to taste
1 T. all-purpose flour
½ c. barbecue sauce

1 onion, thinly sliced
4 potatoes, peeled and cubed
1 T. vegetable oil
2 t. chili powder

Arrange pork chops without overlapping on a large sheet of aluminum foil. Sprinkle with salt and pepper to taste. In a small bowl, stir flour into barbecue sauce; spoon over pork chops. Arrange onion slices over top. In a medium bowl, toss together potatoes, oil and chili powder; arrange in an even layer over onion slices. Seal foil package tightly. Place on grill; cover and cook over medium-high heat 25 to 30 minutes. Makes 6 servings.

Diana Chaney
Olathe, KS

Jambo

Not quite gumbo and not quite jambalaya, this dish is great with cornbread.

3 c. Kielbasa sausage, thinly
   sliced
28-oz. can diced tomatoes
3 c. water
2 zucchini, halved and sliced
½ c. okra, sliced

½ c. green beans, cut into
   2-inch pieces
2 bay leaves
hot pepper sauce to taste
3 to 4 c. cooked rice

Brown sausage. Combine all ingredients except hot pepper sauce and rice in a stockpot; bring to a boil. Reduce heat and simmer 20 to 25 minutes; remove and discard bay leaves. Add hot pepper sauce to taste; serve over cooked rice. Makes 4 servings.

Megan Brooks
Antioch, TN

Grilled Sausage & Veggies

Vickie (Gooseberry Patch)

1½ lbs. green beans, trimmed
1 lb. redskin potatoes, quartered
1 to 2 sweet onions, sliced
28 oz. smoked sausage, cut into
   1-inch pieces

1 t. salt
1 t. pepper
1 T. butter, sliced
½ c. water

Arrange beans, potatoes and onions on a large sheet of aluminum foil; top with sausage. Add salt and pepper; dot with butter. Bring up aluminum foil around ingredients; sprinkle with water and close tightly. Place packets on a hot grill; cover and cook 30 to 45 minutes, turning once, until sausage is browned and vegetables are tender. Serves 4.

Cheesy Sausage-Potato Casserole

J.J. Presley (Portland, TX)

Add some fresh green beans too, if you like.

3 to 4 potatoes, sliced
14 oz. smoked sausage, sliced into
   2-inch lengths
1 onion, chopped

½ c. butter, sliced
1 c. shredded Cheddar cheese
Garnish: chopped green onions

Layer potatoes, sausage and onion in a 13"x9" baking pan sprayed with non-stick vegetable spray. Dot with butter; sprinkle with cheese. Bake, uncovered, at 350 degrees for 1½ hours. Garnish with green onions. Serves 6 to 8.

Smoky Sausage Stew

Add a little hot pepper sauce, if you like.

14½-oz. can beef broth, divided
14½-oz. can stewed tomatoes
16-oz. pkg. smoked bratwurst, sliced
4 new potatoes, cubed
2 onions, coarsely chopped
1 c. baby carrots
¼ c. all-purpose flour
1 green pepper, diced

Set aside ¼ cup beef broth. Combine remaining beef broth, tomatoes, bratwurst, potatoes, onions and carrots in a large stockpot over medium heat. Bring to a boil; reduce heat and simmer 15 to 20 minutes, until vegetables are tender. In a small bowl, combine reserved broth with flour, stirring until smooth; stir into pot until stew is thickened. Add green pepper; simmer 3 minutes. Serves 6.

Marlene Darnell
Newport Beach, CA

Creamy Ham + Noodles

3 c. water
1 T. chicken bouillon granules
8-oz. pkg. wide egg noodles, uncooked
1 c. frozen mixed vegetables
⅓ c. onion, chopped
10¾-oz. can cream of mushroom soup
1 c. shredded Cheddar cheese
½ c. milk
2 c. cooked ham, cubed
¼ t. pepper

simple swap

This dish is equally good made with chicken as it is with ham.

Bring water and bouillon to a boil in a medium stockpot. Stir in noodles; reduce heat, cover and simmer 5 minutes, stirring occasionally. Add mixed vegetables and onion. Cover and simmer an additional 5 minutes or until noodles are tender and most of the liquid is absorbed. Add soup, cheese and milk; mix well. Stir in ham and pepper; heat through. Serves 6.

Colleen Lambert
Casco, WI

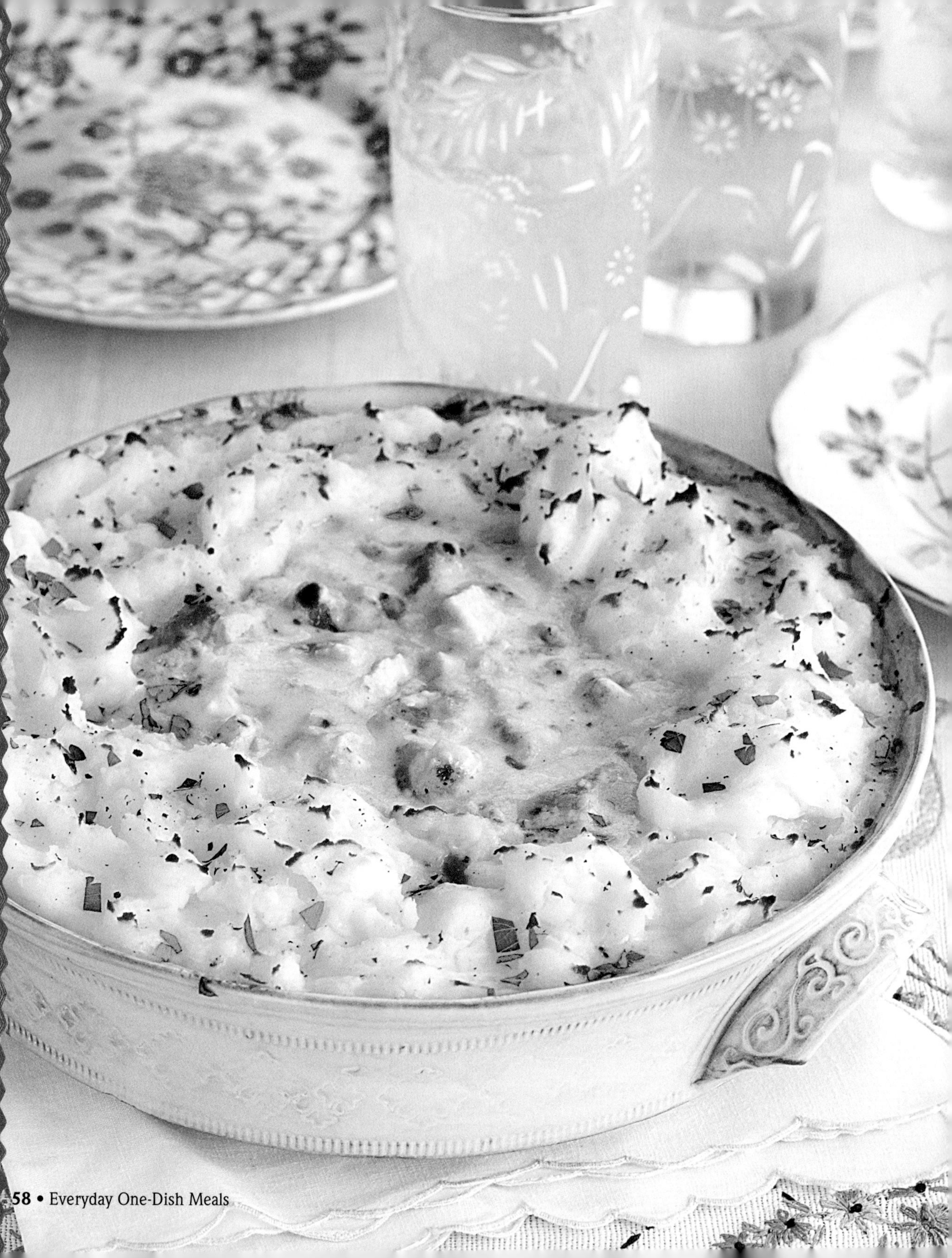

Ham & Potato Casserole

Prepared or mashed potatoes can also be used in this recipe.

1 c. green pepper, chopped
½ c. onion, chopped
¼ c. butter
10¾-oz. can cream of
   mushroom soup
¾ c. milk

1 T. mustard
½ t. pepper
5 c. cooked ham, cubed
24-oz. pkg. refrigerated
   mashed potatoes
Garnish: minced fresh parsley

Sauté green pepper and onion in butter in a large skillet over medium-high heat 5 minutes, or until tender; add remaining ingredients except mashed potatoes and parsley. Bring to a boil; remove from heat and pour into a greased 2-quart casserole dish. Arrange mashed potatoes in a ring on top. Bake, uncovered, at 350 degrees for 20 minutes. Garnish with parsley. Serves 6.

Sally Jukola
Manitou Springs, CO

take-along tips

Bake this casserole ahead and wrap it tightly with aluminum foil. Transport it using a casserole tote. Or you may also bake the casserole once you arrive at your gathering.

gotta love leftovers

This recipe is a perfect way to use leftover ham. If your family loves cheese, you can also use cheesy mashed potatoes or stir cheese into the mashed potatoes before baking.

Reuben Tossed Salad

"This salad was always a big hit at our son's scouting banquets. When I'm short on time, I pick up ingredients from the grocery store's salad bar and add bottles of Thousand Island salad dressing."

—Sally

27-oz. can sauerkraut, drained and rinsed
1 c. carrots, peeled and grated
1 c. green pepper, chopped
8-oz. pkg. sliced Swiss cheese, cut into thin strips

8-oz. pkg. deli corned beef, thinly sliced and cut into thin strips
2 slices rye bread, toasted, buttered and cubed

In a large bowl, mix together all ingredients; toss with Dressing. Serves 6 to 8.

Dressing:

½ c. mayonnaise
2 t. chili sauce

1 T. milk
onion to taste, chopped

Combine all ingredients in a small bowl; mix well.

Sally Bourdlaies
Bay City, MI

Chicken-Pepper Pasta

6 T. butter
1 onion, chopped
1 red pepper, sliced
1 yellow pepper, sliced
1 t. garlic, minced
3 lbs. boneless, skinless chicken breasts, cut into strips
1 t. fresh tarragon, minced

¾ t. salt
¼ t. pepper
¾ c. half-and-half
1 c. shredded mozzarella cheese
½ c. grated Parmesan cheese
8-oz. pkg. vermicelli, cooked
Garnish: fresh tarragon

"My husband and I love this dish. The aroma is wonderful!"

—Pamela

In a skillet, melt butter over medium-high heat until sizzling; stir in onion, peppers and garlic. Cook over medium-high heat until peppers are crisp-tender, 2 to 3 minutes. Remove vegetables from skillet with a slotted spoon and set aside. Add chicken, tarragon, salt and pepper to skillet. Continue cooking, stirring occasionally, until chicken is golden and tender, 7 to 9 minutes. Add vegetables, half-and-half and cheeses to chicken mixture. Reduce heat to medium; continue heating until cheese has melted, 3 to 5 minutes. Add vermicelli; toss gently to coat. Garnish, if desired. Serve immediately. Serves 4 to 6.

Pamela Chorney
Providence Forge, VA

Grilled Chicken + Veggies

Make as many packages as you have guests…good served over rice.

1 boneless, skinless chicken breast
½ c. red pepper, sliced
1 carrot, peeled and sliced
1 c. broccoli flowerets
½ c. onion, halved and sliced
salt and pepper to taste

Arrange chicken and vegetables on a large sheet of aluminum foil; add salt and pepper to taste. Close aluminum foil tightly; place packet on hot grill. Cover and cook over medium-high heat 15 to 25 minutes, turning frequently, until juices run clear when chicken is pierced. Serves one.

Deb Powers
Ankeny, IA

Oh-So-Easy Chicken + Veggies

Try this recipe with three turkey thighs, sweet potatoes and a bit of dried sage too.

2 T. all-purpose flour
2.6-oz. pkg. golden onion soup mix
1 c. water
3 carrots, peeled and diced
2 redskin potatoes, cut into wedges
1 green pepper, cubed
6 boneless, skinless chicken breasts
seasoned salt to taste
pepper to taste

Shake flour in a large oven bag; arrange bag in a 13"x9" baking pan. Add soup mix and water to bag; squeeze bag to blend in flour. Add carrots, potatoes and green pepper; turn bag to coat ingredients. Sprinkle chicken with seasoned salt and pepper to taste; arrange in bag on top of vegetables. Close bag with nylon tie provided; cut six ½-inch slits in top. Tuck ends of bag into pan. Bake at 350 degrees for 55 to 60 minutes, until chicken is tender and juices run clear when chicken is pierced. Serves 6.

Laura Fuller
Fort Wayne, IN

Momma's Divine Divan

Choose rotisserie chicken from your supermarket deli to add more flavor to this family favorite. Generally, one rotisserie chicken will yield 3 cups of chopped meat, so you'll need 2 rotisserie chickens to get the 4 to 5 cups needed for this recipe. Add cooked rice, and you have a complete meal!

½ lb. broccoli flowerets, cooked
4 to 5 boneless, skinless chicken breasts, cooked and cubed
salt to taste
1 c. seasoned bread crumbs

1 T. butter, melted
10¾-oz. can cream of chicken soup
½ c. mayonnaise
1 t. curry powder
½ t. lemon juice
1 c. shredded Cheddar cheese

Arrange broccoli in the bottom of a lightly greased 13"x9" baking pan. Sprinkle chicken with salt to taste; place on top of broccoli and set aside. In a small bowl, toss together bread crumbs and butter. Combine soup, mayonnaise, curry powder and lemon juice in another small bowl; spread over chicken and broccoli. Top with cheese; sprinkle with bread crumb mixture. Bake, uncovered, at 350 degrees for 25 minutes. Serves 8 to 10.

Margaret Vinci
Pasadena, CA

go nuts

You can also add almonds to this dish to add a little extra crunch. Toast sliced or slivered almonds on the stovetop before adding, or just toss them in untoasted.

Mushroom-Garlic-Chicken Pizza

"This recipe gets a big 'YUM' at our house...try it! It's a great way to use left-over baked or grilled chicken too."

—Judy

12-inch Italian pizza crust
¾ c. ranch salad dressing
2 T. garlic, minced
1 chicken breast, cooked and sliced
2 4-oz. cans sliced mushrooms, drained

salt and pepper to taste
8-oz. pkg. shredded mozzarella cheese
Optional: fresh oregano leaves, red pepper flakes

Place crust on an ungreased pizza pan or baking sheet. Spread salad dressing and garlic on crust. Arrange sliced chicken and mushrooms on top. Add salt and pepper to taste; cover with cheese. Bake at 400 degrees for 8 to 10 minutes, until cheese melts. Cut into wedges. Garnish with oregano and red pepper flakes, if desired. Serves 6 to 8.

Judy Davis
Muskogee, OK

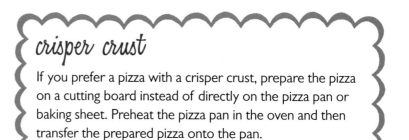

crisper crust

If you prefer a pizza with a crisper crust, prepare the pizza on a cutting board instead of directly on the pizza pan or baking sheet. Preheat the pizza pan in the oven and then transfer the prepared pizza onto the pan.

Honey Chicken Stir-Fry

Measure out the seasonings before you begin to stir-fry…you'll find this dish comes together very quickly.

2 lbs. boneless, skinless
   chicken breasts, cut into
   bite-size pieces
¼ c. honey, divided
1 egg, beaten
⅓ c. plus 1 T. water, divided
1 t. Worcestershire sauce
½ t. dried thyme
¼ t. lemon-pepper seasoning

¼ t. garlic powder
⅛ t. dried oregano
⅛ t. dried marjoram
2 T. vegetable oil
1 T. cornstarch
14-oz. pkg. frozen stir-fry
   vegetables
¼ t. salt
cooked rice

In a large bowl, combine chicken, 2 tablespoons honey, egg, ⅓ cup water, Worcestershire sauce and seasonings; set aside. Heat oil in a wok or large skillet over medium-high heat. Add chicken; cook, stirring frequently, until golden. Remove chicken from wok; keep warm. In a small bowl, mix cornstarch with remaining 2 tablespoons honey and one tablespoon water; set aside. Add vegetables to wok; sprinkle with salt. Cook over medium-high heat 6 to 8 minutes, or until vegetables begin to thaw; drizzle with cornstarch mixture. Continue cooking 6 minutes, or until vegetables are tender; stir in chicken and heat through. Serve with rice. Serves 4 to 6.

Lynn Ruble
Decatur, IN

Grecian Chicken

8 boneless, skinless chicken breasts
8 to 10 potatoes, peeled and quartered
8 to 10 carrots, peeled
2 T. dried rosemary
3 T. olive oil
3 T. lemon juice
salt and pepper to taste
1 t. garlic powder
Garnish: fresh rosemary

Place chicken in a greased roasting pan; bake, uncovered, at 450 degrees until golden, about 20 minutes. Add potatoes and carrots to pan; pour in enough water to partially cover vegetables. Sprinkle with dried rosemary; drizzle with oil and lemon juice. Sprinkle with salt, pepper and garlic powder. Reduce oven temperature to 350 degrees. Cover and bake about 3 hours, or until vegetables are tender. Garnish with fresh rosemary. Serves 8.

Lisa Hains
Tipp City, OH

Baked Chicken Reuben

How clever…our favorite deli sandwich flavors in a casserole!

4 boneless, skinless chicken breasts
¼ t. salt
⅛ t. pepper
2 c. sauerkraut, drained
8-oz. bottle Russian salad dressing
4 slices Swiss cheese
1 T. dried parsley
Garnish: fresh chives, chopped

Arrange chicken breasts in an ungreased 13"x9" baking pan; sprinkle with salt and pepper. Spread sauerkraut over chicken; pour dressing evenly over all. Top with cheese slices and parsley; cover and bake at 350 degrees for one hour, or until tender. Sprinkle with chives. Serves 4.

Doris Reichard
Baltimore, MD

Pixie's Chicken Casserole

Pixie's Chicken Casserole

4 c. cooked chicken, cubed
2 c. celery, diced
2 10¾-oz. cans cream of
　chicken soup
1½ c. mayonnaise
2 c. cooked rice
1 T. dried, minced onion
salt and pepper to taste
1 c. cashew halves
2 c. chow mein noodles

Combine all ingredients except cashews and noodles in a lightly greased 3-quart casserole dish. Top with cashews and noodles; bake, uncovered, at 375 degrees for 40 minutes. Serves 6 to 8.

Kelly Elliott
Burns, TN

"Pixie is a dear family friend who served this easy-yet-elegant dish at a bridal luncheon in my honor."
—Kelly

Frank's Chicken

The mouthwatering gravy is tasty over rice.

4 potatoes, peeled and
　quartered
1 carrot, peeled and chopped
1 onion, diced
1 stalk celery, chopped
6 to 8 chicken legs and thighs
½ c. chicken broth
¼ c. white wine or chicken
　broth
2 t. garlic powder
1½ t. paprika
½ t. dried rosemary
½ t. dried basil
Optional: 2 to 3 T. cornstarch

Place vegetables in bottom of a 5-quart slow cooker; arrange chicken on top. Pour chicken broth and wine or additional broth over all; sprinkle with seasonings. Cover and cook on low setting for 8 hours or on high setting for 5 hours. Remove chicken and vegetables to a serving platter. If desired, stir cornstarch into juices in slow cooker until thickened to make gravy. Serves 4 to 6.

Tricia Roberson
Indian Head, MD

Spicy Sausage & Chicken Creole

"I used this dish to win over my husband and his family while we were dating. He likes his food spicy! Of course, you can use a little less hot pepper sauce, if you prefer."

–Carrie

14½-oz. can diced tomatoes
½ c. long-cooking rice, uncooked
½ c. hot water
2 t. hot pepper sauce
¼ t. garlic powder
¼ t. dried oregano
16-oz. pkg. frozen broccoli, green bean & red pepper blend, thawed

4 boneless, skinless chicken thighs
8-oz. link Italian sausage, cooked and quartered
8-oz. can tomato sauce
Garnish: chopped fresh parsley

Combine tomatoes, rice, water, hot pepper sauce and seasonings in an ungreased 13"x9" baking pan. Cover and bake at 375 degrees for 10 minutes. Stir in vegetables; top with chicken and sausage. Pour tomato sauce over top. Bake, covered, at 375 degrees for 40 minutes, or until juices run clear when chicken is pierced. Garnish with parsley. Serves 4.

Carrie Knotts
Kalispell, MT

Turkey-Spinach Quiches

1 lb. ground turkey sausage, browned and drained
3 c. shredded Cheddar cheese
10-oz. pkg. frozen chopped spinach, cooked and drained
6.5-oz. jar sliced mushrooms, drained
⅔ c. onion, chopped
1 c. mayonnaise
1 c. milk
4 eggs, beaten
1¼ c. biscuit baking mix
2 T. cornstarch

In a large bowl, mix together all ingredients. Pour into greased mini pie tins. Bake, uncovered, at 350 degrees for 20 minutes, or until golden and set. Serves 4 to 6.

"This recipe is a holiday tradition at our house. I bake it in mini pie tins for a nice presentation…my guests love it."
—Jenny

Jenny Poole
Salisbury, NC

Rita's Turkey Hash

"This is my favorite hearty breakfast to serve every Black Friday, before my sisters and I head to the mall to do some serious shopping. Add a side of leftover cranberry sauce...delish!"

—Rita

1 T. butter
1 T. vegetable oil
1 onion, chopped
1 red pepper, chopped
2 c. potatoes, peeled, cooked and diced

2 c. roast turkey, diced
1 t. fresh thyme
salt and pepper to taste

Melt butter with oil in a large, heavy skillet over medium heat. Add onion and red pepper. Sauté until onion is tender, about 5 minutes. Add remaining ingredients. Spread out mixture in skillet, pressing lightly to form an even layer. Cook 5 to 10 minutes, or until golden. Remove from heat. Spoon hash onto 4 plates. Top with Poached Eggs and serve immediately. Serves 4.

Poached Eggs:

1 T. white vinegar
4 eggs

salt and pepper to taste

Add several inches of water to a deep skillet or saucepan. Bring water to a simmer over medium-high heat. Stir in vinegar. Crack eggs, one at a time, into water. Cook just until whites are firm and yolks are still soft, about 3 to 4 minutes. Remove eggs with a slotted spoon. Sprinkle with salt and pepper.

Rita Morgan
Pueblo, CO

Shrimp Pasta Salad

1½ c. cooked elbow macaroni
1 lb. frozen cooked tiny
   shrimp, thawed
1 c. frozen green peas, thawed
1 red pepper, sliced
1 c. mayonnaise

2 eggs, hard-boiled, peeled and
   diced
2 T. onion, minced
seasoned salt and pepper to
   taste

Rinse macaroni in cold water. Drain macaroni, shrimp and peas well; combine in a large bowl and set aside. Chop red pepper in a blender. Add mayonnaise and blend until the mayonnaise turns pink; set aside. Add eggs and onion to shrimp mixture; stir in mayonnaise mixture. Sprinkle with seasoned salt and pepper. Serves 4.

Debra Donaldson
Florala, AL

"This cool, refreshing salad is scrumptious! I serve it with sliced cheese, crackers, fresh fruit and sweet tea."

—Debra

Bread, Crab + Shrimp Salad

Use all shrimp or all crab, if you prefer.

1 loaf French bread, crusts
   trimmed
4 to 5 eggs, hard-boiled, peeled
   and diced
1 onion, diced
1½ lbs. frozen cooked tiny
   shrimp, thawed
1½ lbs. crabmeat, cooked

1 c. celery, diced
3 c. mayonnaise-type salad
   dressing
1 t. seasoned salt flavor
   enhancer
Garnish: lettuce leaves,
   paprika

Cube bread; combine with eggs and onion in a large bowl. Cover and refrigerate overnight. Add remaining ingredients except lettuce and paprika. Cover and refrigerate overnight. Serve over lettuce leaves. Sprinkle with paprika. Serves 4 to 6.

Debbie Meyer
Sacramento, CA

Shrimp & Wild Rice

To save time, have the seafood department steam the shrimp for you. They'll need to start with ¾ pound of unpeeled raw shrimp.

make-ahead magic

Prepare this casserole a day in advance, then wrap the baking pan tightly with aluminum foil or plastic wrap. Refrigerate overnight; bake the casserole before serving.

6-oz. pkg. long-grain and wild rice mix, uncooked
1 yellow onion, chopped
1 green pepper, chopped
½ c. butter
8-oz. pkg. sliced mushrooms
1 t. hot pepper sauce

salt and pepper to taste
1 c. heavy cream
½ lb. cooked, peeled and cleaned medium shrimp
¼ c. slivered or sliced almonds

Prepare wild rice mix according to package directions. Sauté onion and green pepper in butter in a large skillet until tender. Stir in mushrooms, hot pepper sauce and salt and pepper to taste; remove from heat. Add cream and cooked rice; cool slightly. Add shrimp, mixing well. Pour into a buttered 11"x7" baking pan; top with almonds. Bake, uncovered, at 350 degrees for 30 minutes. Serves 4.

Teresa Mulhern
Powell, OH

for the holidays

You can also consider making this rice and serving it as a side dish for the holidays or a special occasion. To do this, you might want to cut the shrimp into smaller pieces before baking.

Shrimp Kabobs

Shrimp Kabobs

Ready to eat in minutes!

3 carrots, cut diagonally
1 green pepper, cut into 1-inch
  strips
¼ c. water
½ t. orange zest

½ c. orange juice
2 t. fresh thyme, minced
2 t. canola oil
12 to 16 uncooked large
  shrimp, peeled and cleaned

Combine carrots, green pepper and water in a saucepan. Bring to a boil; reduce heat, cover and simmer 3 minutes. In a small bowl, combine orange zest, orange juice, thyme and oil. Set aside. Lightly grease grill or broiler pan. Thread shrimp, carrots and peppers on skewers; place on grill. Baste kabobs with orange juice mixture and grill 3 inches from heat for 2 minutes. Turn kabobs, baste and grill another 3 minutes, or until shrimp turn pink. Serves 4.

make-ahead magic

Prepare the kabobs a day in advance and refrigerate overnight before grilling.

Shrimp Creole

If your family likes Spanish rice, they'll love this delicious seafood variation.

1 c. onion, chopped
1 c. green pepper, chopped
1 c. celery, sliced
2 cloves garlic, minced
¼ c. butter
¼ c. all-purpose flour
1 t. salt

pepper to taste
1 bay leaf
14.5-oz. can diced tomatoes
1½ lbs. uncooked shrimp,
  peeled and cleaned
3 to 4 c. cooked rice

Sauté onion, green pepper, celery and garlic in butter in a skillet over medium heat 6 minutes, or until tender. Blend in flour; stir until golden. Add salt, pepper and bay leaf; stir in tomatoes until sauce is thickened. Reduce heat to low; add shrimp. Cover and simmer 10 minutes, or just until shrimp are pink, stirring occasionally. Discard bay leaf; serve over cooked rice. Serves 6 to 8.

Kathy Grashoff
Fort Wayne, IN

Scallops + Shrimp with Linguine

Everyone will love this!

3 T. butter or margarine, divided
3 T. olive oil, divided
1 lb. uncooked large shrimp, peeled and cleaned
3 cloves garlic, minced and divided
1 lb. uncooked sea scallops
8-oz. pkg. sliced mushrooms
2 c. snow peas, trimmed
2 tomatoes, chopped
½ c. green onions, chopped
1 t. salt
½ t. red pepper flakes
¼ c. fresh parsley, chopped
2 T. fresh basil, chopped
10 oz. linguine, cooked and kept warm
grated Parmesan cheese

Heat one tablespoon each of butter or margarine and olive oil in a large skillet over medium-high heat. Add shrimp and half of garlic; cook 2 to 3 minutes, until shrimp turn pink. Remove shrimp from skillet; keep warm. Repeat with scallops, one tablespoon butter or margarine, one table-spoon oil and remaining garlic. Heat remaining one tablespoon each of butter or margarine and oil in same skillet over medium heat. Add mush-rooms, snow peas, tomatoes, green onions, salt, pepper flakes, parsley, and basil; cook 4 to 5 minutes. Combine linguine, mushroom mixture, shrimp and scallops in a large bowl; toss well. Sprinkle with Parmesan cheese. Serves 8.

take-along tips

Prepare this dish in a large serving bowl, then wrap tightly with plastic wrap. Once you arrive at your destination, sprinkle the dish with grated Parmesan cheese.

Cheesy Rotini + Broccoli

Replace the broccoli with asparagus tips for variety.

1½ c. **rotini pasta**, uncooked
2 **carrots**, peeled and sliced
1 c. **broccoli flowerets**
10¾-oz. can **Cheddar cheese soup**

½ c. **milk**
½ c. shredded **Cheddar cheese**
1 T. **mustard**

Cook pasta according to package directions. Add carrots and broccoli during last 5 minutes of cooking time; drain and return to saucepan. Stir soup, milk, cheese and mustard into pasta mixture; heat through. Serves 4.

Marian Buckley
Fontana, CA

Rigatoni with Blue Cheese

Feel free to substitute your favorite tube pasta, like penne or mostaccioli.

16-oz. pkg. rigatoni pasta,
  uncooked
2 T. butter
½ c. crumbled blue cheese

2 T. grated Parmesan cheese
pepper to taste
Garnish: chopped fresh parsley

Cook rigatoni according to package directions; drain and return to sauce-pan. Add butter and cheese; stir to mix until melted. Sprinkle with pepper to taste. Garnish with parsley. Serves 4 to 6.

Zoe Bennett
Columbia, SC

Panzanella Bread Salad

This traditional Italian bread salad began as a thrifty way to use up day-old bread. Now we make it just because it's delicious!

take-along tips

This dish is perfect for a potluck or church gathering because it needs to stand at room temperature before being served. Prepare the salad in the serving bowl and wrap tightly with plastic wrap.

4 c. Italian bread, cut into
  bite-size pieces
5 tomatoes, diced
½ red onion, sliced
½ cucumber, peeled,
  quartered and sliced
½ c. fresh basil, chopped

3 cloves garlic, minced
3 T. red wine vinegar
¼ c. olive oil
½ t. salt
pepper to taste
Garnish: small fresh basil leaves

Combine bread, vegetables, chopped basil and garlic in a large bowl; toss well. Sprinkle with vinegar, oil, salt and pepper. Let stand at room temperature 1½ to 2 hours before serving so the bread can absorb the dressing. Garnish with basil leaves. Serves 4 to 6.

Annmarie Heavey
Bridgewater, MA

in season

This is a great dish to make in the summertime to show off all your fresh produce. Because this dish uses so few ingredients, you can really taste the flavors of delicious seasonal produce.

Vegetable Lo Mein à la Rob

Lo mein noodles are usually the key ingredient in this Asian dish, but the "à la Rob" version of this dish substitutes rice noodles. We'll let you choose…it's good either way.

8-oz. pkg. rice noodles, cooked
2 T. plus 1 t. sesame oil, divided
½ t. salt
1 onion, halved and sliced into crescents
2 stalks celery, thinly sliced
2 cloves garlic, pressed
1½ t. fresh ginger, peeled and shredded

1 carrot, peeled and shredded
¼ lb. snow peas
1 c. sliced mushrooms
1 c. frozen corn kernels
Optional: dry white wine or vegetable broth

In a medium bowl, toss noodles with one teaspoon sesame oil and salt; set aside. Heat remaining 2 tablespoons oil in a skillet over high heat. Add onion and next 7 ingredients, one at a time, in order given; stir-fry each 2 to 4 minutes, until crisp-tender. Add a little white wine or vegetable broth to skillet if skillet becomes too dry. Pour noodles on top; reduce heat to low. Drizzle Sauce over noodles and toss together. Serves 4 to 6.

Sauce:

½ c. dry white wine or vegetable broth
¼ c. sugar
1½ T. cornstarch
6 T. soy sauce

4 t. hoisin sauce
2 t. sesame oil
1 t. rice wine vinegar or white vinegar

Combine all ingredients in a small saucepan. Cook over low heat 5 minutes or until thickened. Keep warm. Makes one cup.

Robbin Chamberlain
Worthington, OH

Skillet-Toasted Corn Salad

The corn for this salad is cooked until toasty brown and tossed with peppers and Parmesan cheese...yummy!

⅓ c. plus 1 T. olive oil, divided
⅓ c. lemon juice
1 T. Worcestershire sauce
3 cloves garlic, minced
3 to 4 dashes hot pepper sauce
¼ t. salt
½ t. pepper

6 ears sweet corn, husks and kernels removed
4 red, yellow and green peppers, coarsely chopped
½ c. grated Parmesan cheese
1 head romaine lettuce, cut crosswise into 1-inch pieces

Combine ⅓ cup oil, lemon juice, Worcestershire sauce, garlic, hot pepper sauce, salt and pepper in a jar with a tight-fitting lid. Cover and shake well; set aside. Heat remaining oil in a large skillet over medium-high heat. Add corn kernels; sauté 5 minutes, or until corn is tender and golden, stirring often. Remove from heat. Combine corn, peppers and cheese in a large bowl. Pour dressing over corn mixture; toss lightly to coat. Serve over lettuce. Serves 6 to 8.

Sherri Cooper
Armada, MI

Zucchini Pancakes

You'll love these tender pancakes...they're super for a brunch buffet!

½ c. biscuit baking mix
¼ c. grated Parmesan cheese
salt and pepper to taste
2 eggs, beaten

2 c. zucchini, shredded
oil for frying
Garnish: butter, maple syrup, sour cream

In a medium bowl, combine all ingredients except oil and garnish; stir until mixed. Heat oil in a skillet over medium-high heat. Drop batter by 2 tablespoonfuls into skillet. Cook and flip until golden on both sides. Serve warm; garnish as desired. Serves 4.

Nancy Dearborn
Erie, PA

Easy Southern-Style Pork
Barbecue, page 109

seasonal celebrations

Holiday gatherings don't have to be fancy! Invite family & friends over for a Christmas Eve dinner of Snowy Day Chili or Mock Lasagna Casserole. Celebrate the Fourth of July with Bacon-Stuffed Burgers or Midwest Family Picnic Salad. Enjoy your favorite holidays throughout the year with these delicious recipes.

Christmas Eve
Pot Roast

Christmas Eve Pot Roast

2 t. salt
1 t. paprika
1 t. garlic powder
½ t. pepper
4- to 5-lb. boneless chuck roast
3 T. all-purpose flour
2 T. vegetable oil
⅔ c. water

2 bay leaves
3 onions, quartered
5 carrots, peeled, quartered
4 potatoes, peeled, quartered
14½-oz. can Italian-style diced
    tomatoes, undrained
15-oz. can tomato sauce
Garnish: fresh rosemary

"This is the best pot roast I have ever made! It's easy, and it fills the house with the most wonderful mouthwatering aroma."
—Kristine

Blend seasonings in a small bowl; rub into roast and coat with flour. Heat oil in a heavy saucepan; add roast and brown on all sides over high heat. Add water and bay leaves; cover, reduce heat to low and simmer 3 hours. Add remaining ingredients, cover and simmer one hour. Discard bay leaves. Garnish with rosemary. Serves 6 to 8.

Kristine Marumoto
Sandy, UT

Boycott-Your-Grill Beef Kabobs

1 c. olive oil
⅔ c. soy sauce
½ c. lemon juice
¼ c. Worcestershire sauce
¼ c. mustard
2 cloves garlic, minced
1 T. pepper
⅛ t. hot pepper sauce

3 lbs. beef sirloin steak, cut
    into 2-inch cubes
2 green peppers, cut into
    1-inch squares
2 8-oz. pkgs. mushrooms
20-oz. can pineapple chunks,
    drained

Combine all ingredients except steak, vegetables and pineapple in a small bowl. Place steak in a large dish. Pour marinade over steak; cover and refrigerate 24 hours. Thread steak, vegetables and pineapple onto skewers. Arrange on greased baking sheets. Bake at 400 degrees for 8 to 10 minutes. Turn and continue baking until steak is done. Serves 4 to 6.

Kathy Solka
Ishpeming, MI

Beef Stroganoff

With tender meat that's cooked with mushrooms and combined with a sour cream sauce, this recipe is perfect for the holiday table. Spoon over a heap of homestyle egg noodles to serve.

¼ c. all-purpose flour
1 t. paprika
½ t. salt
¼ t. pepper
1-lb. boneless sirloin steak, cubed
¼ c. butter

2 cloves garlic, minced
1 c. beef broth
½ c. water
2 c. sliced mushrooms
½ c. sour cream
hot cooked egg noodles

Combine flour, paprika, salt and pepper in a plastic zipping bag; add steak, shaking to coat. Melt butter in a 12" skillet over medium heat; brown steak with garlic in butter. Add broth, water and mushrooms; mix well. Bring to a boil; reduce heat, cover and simmer 30 minutes, or until meat is tender. Uncover and simmer 10 minutes, or until thickened. Stir in sour cream; heat thoroughly (do not boil). Serve over hot cooked egg noodles. Serves 4.

Elizabeth Watters
Edwardsville, IL

mix it up

While beef stroganoff typically is served over egg noodles, it can also be served over toasted bread or rice. Round out your meal with a salad, green beans or broccoli.

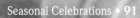

Bacon-Stuffed
Burgers

Sisler Family Spinach Hamburgers

2 lbs. ground beef
10-oz. pkg. frozen chopped
   spinach, thawed
½ to ¾ c. grated Parmesan
   cheese
1.35-oz. pkg. onion soup mix
4 to 6 sandwich buns, split

In a large bowl, combine all ingredients except buns, mixing well with hands. Form into 4 to 6 patties. Place on grill; cover and cook over medium heat to desired doneness. Serve on buns. Makes 4 to 6 servings.

Charlotte Keul
Des Moines, IA

"This recipe has been passed down from my grandmother's family, and was a tradition in my home when I was growing up. Now I serve it to my family."
—Charlotte

Bacon-Stuffed Burgers

4 slices bacon, crisply cooked
   and crumbled, drippings
   reserved
¼ c. onion, chopped
4-oz. can mushroom pieces,
   drained and diced
1 lb. ground beef
1 lb. ground pork sausage
¼ c. grated Parmesan cheese
½ t. pepper
½ t. garlic powder
2 T. steak sauce
8 sandwich buns, split
Optional: lettuce leaves,
   tomato slices, provolone
   cheese slices

Heat 2 tablespoons reserved bacon drippings in a skillet over medium heat. Add onion and sauté until tender. Add bacon and mushrooms; heat through and set aside. Combine beef, sausage, Parmesan cheese, pepper, garlic powder and steak sauce in a large bowl. Shape into 16 patties. Spoon bacon mixture over 8 patties. Place remaining patties on top and press edges tightly to seal. Grill over medium coals to desired doneness. Serve on buns with lettuce, tomato and cheese, if desired. Makes 8.

Molly Cool
Delaware, OH

"These go so fast that I have to double the recipe."
—Molly

Easy Gumbo Meatballs

After baking, keep these warm in a slow cooker…they're a potluck favorite!

2 lbs. ground beef
4 slices bread, crumbled
¾ c. evaporated milk
10¾-oz. can chicken gumbo soup
10½-oz. can French onion soup
hot cooked rice
Optional: chopped fresh parsley

Combine ground beef, crumbled bread and evaporated milk in a large bowl; form into one-inch balls. Arrange in an ungreased 13"x9" baking pan; pour soups on top. Bake, uncovered, at 350 degrees for 1½ hours. Serve over cooked rice. Garnish with parsley, if desired. Serves 6.

Brenda Flowers
Olney, IL

make-ahead magic

Prepare this recipe completely the night before and store, tightly wrapped, in the baking pan overnight. Bake it in the oven the next evening for dinner.

Snowy Day Chili

2 lbs. ground beef or venison
2 c. onion, chopped
4 c. tomato sauce
4 c. water
15-oz. can kidney beans,
 drained and rinsed
6-oz. can tomato paste
¼ c. Worcestershire sauce
2 T. brown sugar, packed

1 T. seasoned salt
1 T. lemon juice
3 bay leaves
chili powder to taste
Optional: hot pepper sauce to
 taste
Garnish: shredded Cheddar
 cheese, chopped onion, sour
 cream, corn chips

"In Wisconsin, snow is inevitable, but shoveling sidewalks isn't so dreaded when there's a pot of chili simmering on the stove!"

—Kathie

Brown meat in a large stockpot over medium heat; drain. Stir in remaining ingredients except garnish. Reduce heat; simmer 3 to 4 hours, stirring occasionally. Garnish as desired. Serves 8 to 10.

Kathie Poritz
Burlington, WI

Feliz Navidad Casserole

1½ lbs. ground beef
1 onion, chopped
10¾-oz. can cream of
  chicken soup
10-oz. can red enchilada sauce
4-oz. can diced green chiles
2 t. ground cumin
½ t. salt

½ t. pepper
3 c. shredded Mexican-blend
  or Monterey Jack cheese,
  divided
10 8-inch flour tortillas,
  divided
Garnish: chopped tomatoes,
  sliced green onions

Brown ground beef and onion in a large skillet over medium heat; drain. Stir in soup, enchilada sauce, green chiles, cumin, salt and pepper; simmer 10 minutes. Spread one-third of meat sauce in a greased 13"x9" baking pan. Sprinkle with one cup cheese. Add a layer of tortillas, tearing tortillas to fit pan and completely covering the beef mixture and cheese. Repeat layers, ending with remaining beef mixture and cheese. Bake, uncovered, at 350 degrees for 20 minutes, or until bubbly and cheese is melted. Garnish with tomatoes and green onions. Serves 8.

Tracee Summins
Amarillo, TX

"More than 20 years ago, my husband and I were newlyweds attending college in Lubbock, Texas. I clipped the original recipe for this casserole out of the local newspaper. I've changed it over the years to include our family's favorite ingredients. It's a real winner!"

—Tracee

festive get-together

This is the perfect casserole to serve during the busy holiday season. It can be made in advance, and you can bake it while you mingle with your guests. Serve it with chips and salsa or cheese dip and a big salad for a festive gathering.

Mom's One-Pot Pork Chop Dinner

1 T. butter
4 pork chops
3 potatoes, peeled and sliced
2 c. baby carrots
1 squash, sliced

1 onion, sliced
10¾-oz. can cream of mushroom soup
¼ c. water
Garnish: chopped fresh parsley

Melt butter in a skillet over medium heat and brown pork chops 3 to 5 minutes on each side. Add potatoes, carrots, squash and onion to skillet. Combine soup and water in a small bowl; pour over meat and vegetables. Cover and simmer 15 to 20 minutes, until vegetables are tender. Makes 4 servings.

Kim Allen
New Albany, IN

Pork Chops + Stuffing

take-along tips

Prepare pork chops and stuffing completely, but do not bake. Package tightly in casserole dish. Bake the casserole when you arrive at your destination before serving.

6 pork chops
1 T. shortening
1 t. salt, divided
1 c. celery, chopped
¾ c. onion, chopped
¼ c. butter
¼ c. brown sugar, packed

5 c. bread, cubed
1 egg, beaten
1 t. dried sage
½ t. dried thyme
⅛ t. pepper
11-oz. can mandarin oranges, drained

Brown pork chops in shortening in a skillet over medium heat; remove to a platter and season with ½ teaspoon salt. Lightly brown vegetables in butter in skillet; stir in brown sugar. Combine bread cubes, egg, sage, thyme, pepper and remaining ½ teaspoon salt in a bowl; add to vegetables. Gently stir in oranges. Spoon stuffing into the center of an ungreased 3½-quart casserole dish. Place pork chops around the stuffing and cover with aluminum foil. Bake at 350 degrees for 30 minutes; uncover and bake 30 more minutes. Serves 6.

Barbara Schmeckpeper
Elwood, IL

Cheesy Sausage-Zucchini Casserole

1 lb. ground pork sausage
¼ c. onion, chopped
1 c. tomato, diced
4 c. zucchini, cubed
2 4.5-oz. cans sliced
  mushrooms, drained
1½ c. cooked rice
8-oz. pkg. pasteurized process
  cheese spread, cubed
⅛ t. dried oregano
salt and pepper to taste

Cook and stir sausage and onion in a large skillet over medium heat until evenly browned; drain. Stir in tomato and zucchini; cook until tender. Stir in remaining ingredients and spread in an ungreased 3-quart casserole dish. Bake, uncovered, at 350 degrees for one hour, or until bubbly. Makes 8 servings.

Linda Behling
Cecil, PA

"What fond memories I have of my mom, dad, sister, grandmas and grandpas sitting around the kitchen table and enjoying this scrumptious meal prepared by my mom."
—Linda

Pizza Pasta
Jennifer Clingan (Dayton, OH)

1 lb. ground Italian pork sausage
1 c. onion, chopped
8-oz. pkg. rotini pasta, cooked
8-oz. pkg. sliced mushrooms
4-oz. pkg. sliced pepperoni
15-oz. can pizza sauce
½ green pepper, chopped
2¼-oz. can sliced black olives, drained
8-oz. pkg. shredded mozzarella cheese

Brown sausage and onion in a skillet over medium heat; drain and transfer to an ungreased 3-quart casserole dish. Set aside. Combine pasta, mushrooms, pepperoni, pizza sauce, pepper and olives in a large bowl; spoon over sausage. Sprinkle with cheese; cover and bake at 350 degrees for 45 minutes. Uncover and bake an additional 5 to 10 minutes. Serves 8.

Mock Lasagna Casserole

A tasty twist on an old favorite.

1 lb. ground pork sausage,
  browned and crumbled
15-oz. can tomato sauce
½ t. garlic salt
½ t. pepper
½ t. dried basil
½ c. water
7-oz. pkg. ziti pasta, cooked
1½ c. cottage cheese
6 to 8 slices white American
  cheese, chopped

Combine sausage, sauce, seasonings and water in a medium saucepan over medium heat; cover and simmer 15 minutes, stirring occasionally. In an ungreased 2-quart casserole dish or individual ramekins, layer half each of the pasta, cottage cheese, American cheese and meat sauce; repeat. Bake, uncovered, at 375 degrees for 30 minutes. Makes 4 servings.

Kathy Slevoski
North Hampton, NH

Super Sausage Bread

11-oz. tube refrigerated French
  bread dough
½ lb. ground pork sausage,
  browned and drained
1 c. shredded Cheddar cheese
Optional: pizza sauce, warmed

Roll out dough into a 12-inch circle. Spoon sausage down center; sprinkle with cheese. Fold over sides and ends; pinch together to seal. Place on an ungreased baking sheet. Bake at 350 degrees for 30 to 35 minutes. Cool 30 minutes; slice into 12 pieces. Serve with warm pizza sauce for dipping, if desired. Makes 12 servings.

Tracy Evans
Leesburg, OH

"I make this recipe when my family gets together for our annual Halloween party. We keep the tradition of meeting for every single holiday, even though there are enough of us to fill a gymnasium!"

—Tracy

Swiss and Rye Bites

"These have been on our tailgating menu as long as I can remember. They never last long and are so easy to prepare that I've been known to make extra batches at halftime!"

—Jo Ann

2.8-oz. can French-fried onions, crushed
¾ c. bacon, crisply cooked and crumbled
½ c. mayonnaise
3 c. shredded Swiss cheese
14-oz. jar pizza sauce
1 loaf sliced party rye

Combine onions, bacon, mayonnaise and cheese in a large bowl. Spread one teaspoon pizza sauce on each slice of bread; top with one tablespoon cheese mixture. Arrange on an ungreased baking sheet. Bake at 350 degrees for 12 to 14 minutes, until heated through and cheese is melted. Serves 6.

Jo Ann
Gooseberry Patch

Ham + Potato Scallop

3 T. butter
¼ c. onion, grated
¼ c. green pepper, chopped
3 T. all-purpose flour
1 t. salt
½ t. dry mustard
⅛ t. pepper
1½ c. milk
1 c. shredded sharp Cheddar cheese, divided
5 to 6 potatoes, peeled and sliced
1½ c. cooked ham, diced

Melt butter in a large skillet over medium heat. Add onion and green pepper; cook until tender. Blend in flour and seasonings. Gradually add milk; stir until thickened. Blend in ¾ cup cheese. Layer sliced potatoes, ham and sauce alternately in a greased 2½-quart casserole dish or individual ramekins. Cover and bake at 350 degrees for one hour. Uncover; sprinkle with remaining cheese. Bake, uncovered, an additional 15 minutes, or until potatoes are tender. Serves 4 to 6.

Janet Williams
Santa Ana, CA

Ham & Pineapple Dinner

Stephanie Mayer (Portsmouth, VA)

A great-tasting dinner and a quick fix anytime.

2 T. butter
2½ c. cooked ham, cubed
2 green onions, chopped
1 c. pineapple chunks, drained
1⅓ c. pineapple juice

2 T. brown sugar, packed
2 T. cornstarch
4 t. cider vinegar
2 t. mustard
cooked rice

Melt butter in a large skillet over medium heat. Sauté ham, onions and pineapple in butter about 5 minutes. Combine remaining ingredients except rice in a small bowl. Stir together well and pour over mixture in skillet. Mix well; cook until thickened and heated through, about 5 minutes. Serve over rice. Serves 4.

Ham + Pineapple Kabobs

make-ahead magic

Prepare kabobs completely and marinate in the refrigerator before grilling.

3 lbs. cooked ham, cut into 1-inch chunks
¼ c. soy sauce
¼ c. bourbon
¼ c. dark brown sugar, packed
½ t. ground ginger
fresh pineapple, peeled and cut into chunks

2 or 3 green peppers, cut into chunks
2 or 3 sweet onions, cut into chunks
1 lb. cherry tomatoes
cooked rice

Place ham in a large dish. In a small bowl, combine soy sauce, bourbon, brown sugar and ginger; pour over ham and marinate at least 30 minutes. Reserving marinade, thread ham, pineapple, peppers, onions and tomatoes onto skewers. (Don't forget to soak wooden skewers in water before using them.) Place on a hot grill; cover and cook over medium-high heat, brushing with marinade, about 3 minutes per side, or until vegetables begin to brown. Serve over rice. Serves 4.

Hearty Black-Eyed Peas

Serve these slow-simmered peas plain or with rice and cornbread.

3 c. water
3 c. low-sodium chicken broth
1 onion, chopped
1 smoked ham hock
1 bay leaf
½ t. pepper

Optional: 4 whole jalapeño peppers
16-oz. pkg. dried black-eyed peas
1 t. salt, divided

Combine water, broth, onion, ham hock, bay leaf, pepper and jalapeños, if desired, in a Dutch oven. Bring to a boil; cover, reduce heat and simmer 30 minutes. Rinse and sort peas according to package directions. Add peas and ½ teaspoon salt to Dutch oven; cook, covered, one hour or until peas are tender. If desired, remove meat from ham hock, finely chop and return to Dutch oven. Season with remaining salt. Remove and discard bay leaf. Serves 4 to 6.

Angel Hair Chicken Pasta

Such a tasty pasta dish!

¼ c. butter

0.7-oz. pkg. Italian salad dressing mix

½ c. white wine or chicken broth

10¾-oz. can golden mushroom soup

4-oz. pkg. chive & onion flavored cream cheese

6 boneless, skinless chicken breasts

16-oz. pkg. angel hair pasta, cooked

Garnish: chopped fresh chives

Melt butter in a saucepan over medium heat; add dressing mix, wine or broth and soup. Blend in cream cheese until smooth. Arrange chicken in a greased 13"x9" baking pan; pour mixture over chicken. Bake, uncovered, at 325 degrees for one hour. Serve warm chicken and sauce over hot pasta. Garnish with chives. Serves 6.

Nancy Willis
Farmington Hills, MI

Summery Chicken + Rice Salad

"My mother-in-law shared this wonderful summertime lunch recipe with me years ago. We like to serve it with fresh fruit and homemade banana bread or hard rolls."

–Kay

2 c. cooked chicken breast, cubed
1½ c. cooked rice
½ c. pineapple chunks
2 T. olive oil
1 t. salt

1 c. celery, chopped
¼ c. green pepper, chopped
¾ c. chopped pecans
½ c. to ¾ c. mayonnaise
Garnish: lettuce leaves

Combine chicken, rice, pineapple, oil and salt in a large bowl; cover and chill at least 2 hours. Fold in celery, green pepper and pecans; add mayonnaise to taste. Spoon into a lettuce-lined serving bowl or onto individual serving plates lined with lettuce. Makes 10 to 12 servings.

Kay Johnson
Muskegon, MI

Rosemary-Dijon Chicken Croissants

Pair with fruit salad cups and sweet tea for a delightful brunch.

3 c. cooked chicken breast, chopped
⅓ c. green onions, chopped
Toasted almonds, coarsely chopped
¼ c. plain yogurt
¼ c. mayonnaise
1 t. fresh rosemary, chopped
1 t. Dijon mustard
⅛ t. salt
⅛ t. pepper
Optional: leaf lettuce
10 mini croissants, split

Combine all ingredients except lettuce and croissants in a large bowl; mix well. Arrange lettuce leaves inside croissants, if desired; spread with chicken mixture. Makes 10 mini sandwiches.

Jo Ann
Gooseberry Patch

Susan's Chicken Minis

"I was trying to think of something a little different for lunch when I created these mini sandwiches. Now they're a favorite!"

—Susan

2 T. lemon juice
½ c. mayonnaise
salt to taste
1 t. pepper
3½ c. cooked chicken, finely diced

½ c. celery, finely diced
⅓ c. raisins
⅓ c. chopped walnuts
lettuce leaves
12 mini dinner rolls, split

Combine lemon juice, mayonnaise, salt and pepper in a large bowl. Stir in remaining ingredients except lettuce and rolls. Place lettuce on bottom halves of rolls; top with chicken mixture and top halves of rolls. Makes 12 mini sandwiches.

Susan Brzozowski
Ellicott City, MD

Easy Southern-Style Pork Barbecue

This Southern slow-cooker favorite is also known as pulled-pork barbecue.

3- to 4-lb. pork roast
¼ c. water
2 T. smoke-flavored cooking sauce

pepper to taste
6 to 8 sandwich buns, split
Optional: favorite barbecue sauce, coleslaw

Place pork roast in a 4- to 5-quart slow cooker. Add water; sprinkle evenly with cooking sauce and pepper to taste. Cover and cook on high setting for one hour and then on low setting for 6 to 8 hours. Remove roast from slow cooker; shred meat with a fork. Place meat on buns; top with barbecue sauce and a scoop of coleslaw, if desired. Serves 6 to 8.

Marilyn Morel
Keene, NH

take-along tips

Slow cookers are great for potlucks because they travel well. Prepare the pork completely in the slow cooker and secure the lid to take to your destination. Bring along the buns, coleslaw and barbecue sauce.

Garlicky Chicken + Redskin Potatoes

Roasted chicken with potatoes is a great hearty meal for cold winter days...
what could be better?

8 chicken breasts
3 lbs. redskin potatoes, cut in
half
20 cloves garlic, peeled

1 T. fresh thyme, chopped
salt and pepper to taste
¼ c. olive oil
Optional: fresh thyme sprigs

Place chicken in an ungreased roasting pan. Arrange potatoes and garlic around chicken. Sprinkle with chopped thyme, salt and pepper; drizzle with oil. Bake, uncovered, at 425 degrees for 20 minutes. Reduce oven temperature to 375 degrees. Continue baking 45 minutes to one hour, until chicken is golden and juices run clear when chicken is pierced with a fork. Transfer chicken to a platter. Spoon potatoes and garlic around edges. Garnish with thyme sprigs, if desired. Serves 8.

Vickie
Gooseberry Patch

buy in bulk

Herbs and spices add lots of flavor to food but can be costly at supermarkets. Instead, purchase them at dollar stores, bulk food stores and even ethnic food stores, where they can be quite a bargain.

Chicken + Dressing Bake

2 6-oz. pkgs. cornbread stuffing mix
1 t. dried sage
¼ t. pepper
1 onion, finely chopped
4 stalks celery, finely chopped
2 10¾-oz. cans cream of chicken soup
2 c. chicken broth
2 c. shredded Cheddar cheese, divided
4 boneless, skinless chicken breasts, cooked and cut in half lengthwise

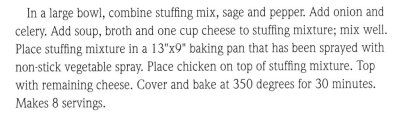

In a large bowl, combine stuffing mix, sage and pepper. Add onion and celery. Add soup, broth and one cup cheese to stuffing mixture; mix well. Place stuffing mixture in a 13"x9" baking pan that has been sprayed with non-stick vegetable spray. Place chicken on top of stuffing mixture. Top with remaining cheese. Cover and bake at 350 degrees for 30 minutes. Makes 8 servings.

Dueley Lucas
Somerset, KY

Fiesta Enchiladas

8-oz. pkg. shredded Cheddar cheese
1 onion, chopped
2-oz. can sliced black olives, drained
1 T. olive oil
24 6-inch corn tortillas
19-oz. can enchilada sauce
4 c. cooked turkey, chopped

Combine cheese, onion and olives; set aside. Heat oil in a skillet over medium heat; add tortillas one at a time and cook until soft. Dip tortillas in sauce. Spoon turkey and cheese mixture into center of each tortilla; roll up and place 12 enchiladas in a lightly greased 13"x9" baking pan. Spread with enough of remaining sauce to cover. Make a second layer of enchiladas; spread remaining sauce on top and sprinkle with remaining cheese mixture. Bake, uncovered, at 350 degrees for 20 minutes, or until cheese is melted. Serves 6.

"A college roommate made this recipe after we'd grown tired of endless turkey sandwiches...what a hit!"

–Nancy

Nancy Ramsey
Delaware, OH

Turnaround Turkey + Rice

A wonderful way to use leftover holiday turkey! Served with steamed broccoli and hot buttered rolls, it's sure to become a family favorite.

2 T. butter
2 stalks celery, chopped
1 onion, chopped
1 c. cooked turkey, cubed
1½ c. water

¼ c. milk
0.87-oz. pkg. turkey gravy mix
2 T. all-purpose flour
1 t. seasoned salt
2 c. cooked long-cooking rice

Melt butter in a saucepan over medium heat. Add celery and onion; cook, stirring frequently, 5 minutes, or until tender. Stir in turkey. Blend together water, milk, gravy mix, flour and salt in a bowl; stir into turkey mixture. Bring to a boil; reduce heat and simmer 5 minutes, or until thickened and heated through. Serve over rice. Makes 2 to 4 servings.

Theresia King
Knoxville, TN

Turkey Meatloaf with Cranberry Glaze

16-oz. can jellied cranberry
  sauce, divided
½ c. chili sauce or catsup
1¼ lbs. lean ground turkey
½ lb. ground pork
1 egg, beaten

1 c. soft bread crumbs
1 onion, finely chopped
¾ t. poultry seasoning
½ t. salt
⅛ t. pepper

"I like to change things up each year for Christmas dinner. I made this recipe last year and discovered it's such a yummy alternative to traditional holiday fare!"

—Penny

In a small bowl, mix together ⅓ cup cranberry sauce and chili sauce or catsup. In a large bowl, combine turkey and remaining ingredients. Add one-third of cranberry sauce mixture. Mix until well blended. Spoon into an 8"x4" loaf pan that has been sprayed lightly with non-stick vegetable spray. Bake, uncovered, at 350 degrees for one hour. Top with remaining cranberry sauce mixture and bake an additional 10 minutes. Let stand 10 minutes before slicing. Serve with remaining cranberry sauce. Serves 6.

Penny Sherman
Cumming, GA

Orange-Pecan Cornish Hens

This recipe is great to make during the busy holiday season…it's perfect served with wild rice.

½ c. butter, melted and divided
4 1½-lb. Cornish game hens
1 t. salt
1 t. pepper

½ c. orange marmalade
¼ c. orange juice
1 t. cornstarch
½ c. chopped pecans
Garnish: orange slices

Spread one tablespoon melted butter evenly over each hen; season with salt and pepper. Tie ends of legs together, if desired, and place on a lightly greased rack in roasting pan. Bake at 400 degrees for one hour, or until a meat thermometer inserted into meaty part of thigh registers 180 degrees. Blend together remaining butter, marmalade and orange juice in a saucepan; bring to a boil. Blend together a small amount of cornstarch and water in a bowl, slowly adding remaining cornstarch until mixture thickens. Slowly add cornstarch mixture to marmalade mixture, stirring constantly; add pecans. Place hens in a greased 15"x10" jelly-roll pan. Pour glaze over hens and bake 10 more minutes, or until glaze begins to turn golden. Garnish with orange slices. Serves 4.

Bubbly Zucchini-Mozzarella Casserole

2 zucchini, sliced
1 yellow squash, sliced
3 4-oz. cans sliced mushrooms, drained
2 14½-oz. cans diced Italian tomatoes with olive oil
Italian seasoning to taste
8-oz. pkg. sliced pepperoni
8-oz. pkg. shredded mozzarella cheese

Layer zucchini and squash in a lightly greased 13"x9" baking pan. Top with mushrooms and tomatoes; sprinkle with Italian seasoning. Top with pepperoni. Cover and bake at 350 degrees for about one hour, or until pepperoni is golden and vegetables are tender. Sprinkle with cheese; bake, uncovered, an additional 10 minutes, or until cheese is melted. Serves 8.

Donna Fannin
Fairfield, OH

"Everyone seems to love this casserole...the combination of flavors just can't be beat."
—Donna

made with love

Food for friends doesn't have to be fancy. Your guests will be delighted with comfort foods like Grandma used to make. Invite them to help themselves from large platters set right on the table. . .so family friendly.

Fresh Lemon Pasta & Basil Sauce

There's nothing like the taste of freshly made pasta.

3 c. all-purpose flour	⅓ c. lemon juice
3 eggs	1 T. olive oil
½ t. salt	2 T. butter

Place flour, eggs and salt in a food processor; cover and pulse until thoroughly combined. Continue to pulse ingredients while adding lemon juice and oil. When dough begins to form, remove from processor and pat into a ball. Cover and allow to rest 20 minutes. Divide dough into quarters. On a lightly floured surface, roll each section of dough into a ⅛-inch thick rectangle. Using a sharp knife or pizza cutter, cut dough into ¼-inch strips, separate noodles and allow to dry 45 minutes to one hour. Fill a large stockpot with water and bring to a boil; add pasta. Bring water to a boil again and cook noodles 10 to 15 minutes, until tender. Drain noodles and toss with butter. Serve with Basil Sauce. Makes 4 servings.

Basil Sauce:

4 tomatoes, chopped	¼ c. fresh cilantro, chopped
½ c. green onions, chopped	2 t. oil
½ c. green pepper, chopped	1 t. white vinegar
⅓ c. fresh basil, chopped	1 clove garlic, minced

In a large bowl with a tight-fitting lid, combine all ingredients and stir until thoroughly combined. Cover bowl with lid and allow flavors to blend one hour. Stir sauce. Refrigerate any leftovers.

Midwest Family Picnic Salad

You can also add diced ham, chicken or tuna...terrific!

16-oz. pkg. rotini pasta,
   cooked
15-oz. can pineapple tidbits,
   drained
1 c. seedless green grapes
1 c. seedless red grapes
1 c. green onions, chopped

1 c. celery, diced
2 carrots, peeled and grated
2 c. mayonnaise
14-oz. can sweetened
   condensed milk
¼ c. sugar
½ c. vinegar

Combine pasta, fruit and vegetables in a large bowl; set aside. In a separate bowl, mix together remaining ingredients until smooth. Add to pasta mixture, tossing to coat. Chill until serving time. Serves 12.

Amy Barthelemy
Eagan, MN

Cheesy Ravioli Bake
Christine Malzone (Totowa, NJ)

A simple, delicious meatless main that you'll love.

2 24-oz. pkgs. frozen mini cheese
   ravioli
1 bunch broccoli, cut into bite-size
   pieces
1 t. garlic powder
¼ c. butter, melted
2 c. shredded mozzarella cheese
Grated Parmesan cheese

Cook ravioli according to package directions; drain. In a separate saucepan, cover broccoli with water. Cook until tender; drain. Stir garlic powder into melted butter. Mix together ravioli, broccoli and butter mixture in a greased 13"x9" baking pan. Sprinkle with mozzarella cheese. Bake, uncovered, at 350 degrees for 20 to 25 minutes, until bubbly and cheese is golden. Sprinkle with Parmesan cheese. Serves 4 to 6.

Angie's Pasta + Sauce

Homemade sauce is so simple to prepare. You'll love the taste of both the sauce and the freshly grated Parmesan on top.

6 to 8 roma tomatoes, halved,
  seeded and diced
1 to 2 cloves garlic, minced
½ c. butter, melted
1 T. dried basil

8-oz. pkg. angel hair pasta,
  cooked
Garnish: freshly grated
  Parmesan cheese

Combine tomatoes and garlic in a saucepan and simmer over medium heat 15 minutes; set aside. Mix together butter and basil in a small bowl; add to pasta in a serving bowl. Toss to coat. Stir in tomato mixture and garnish with cheese. Serves 4 to 6.

Angie Whitmore
Farmington, UT

Whole Acorn Squash Cream Soup

This unique recipe celebrates the beauty of squash by using it as a serving bowl. Choose squash that stand upright for ease in baking and serving.

4 acorn squash	1 c. chicken broth
¼ c. cream cheese	½ t. salt
1 c. whipping cream	1 t. cinnamon

Cut off about one inch of stem ends of squash to reveal seeds. Scoop out and discard seeds and pulp. Arrange squash in an ungreased 13"x9" baking pan. Place one tablespoon cream cheese in each squash. Pour ¼ cup each whipping cream and chicken broth over cream cheese in each squash; sprinkle each with ⅛ teaspoon salt and ¼ teaspoon cinnamon. Add ½ inch of water to baking pan. Bake, uncovered, at 350 degrees for one hour and 45 minutes, or until squash are very tender. To serve, carefully set each squash in a shallow soup bowl. Serves 4.

Lucky-7 Mac & Cheese

"Seven varieties of cheese come together in this favorite home-style dish that stirs up quickly on the stovetop rather than baking in the oven. We consider whoever gets a serving of this...lucky!"

—Tina

1 c. fat-free milk	½ c. provolone cheese, cubed
½ c. extra-sharp Cheddar cheese, cubed	½ c. Monterey Jack cheese, cubed
½ c. Colby cheese, cubed	½ c. crumbled blue cheese
½ c. pasteurized process cheese spread, cubed	16-oz. pkg. elbow macaroni, cooked
½ c. Swiss cheese, cubed	salt and pepper to taste

Cook milk and cheeses in a heavy 4-quart saucepan over low heat until cheeses melt, whisking often. Stir in macaroni; season with salt and pepper. Heat thoroughly. Serves 6 to 8.

Tina Vogel
Orlando, FL

Sunrise Skillet

½ lb. bacon
4 c. potatoes, peeled and
   cubed
½ onion, chopped

6 eggs, beaten
1 c. shredded Cheddar cheese
Chopped green onions

"When our kids want to camp out in the backyard, I just have to wake them to the aroma of a delicious breakfast…and this recipe does the trick every time."
—Melody

Cook bacon in a cast-iron skillet over the slow-burning coals of a camp-fire or on a stove over medium heat until crisply cooked. Remove bacon from skillet; set aside. Stir potatoes and onion into drippings. Cover and cook until potatoes are tender, about 10 to 12 minutes. Crumble bacon into potatoes. Stir in eggs; cover and cook until set, about 2 minutes. Sprinkle with cheese and green onions; let stand until cheese melts. Serves 6 to 8.

Melody Taynor
Everett, WA

Sweet Pea's Breakfast Blitz

> "When I was a young girl, I spent many weekend nights with my Grandma Susie, nicknamed, 'Sweet Pea.' She always served this special breakfast."
>
> —Kimberly

4 eggs
1 to 2 T. cider vinegar
1 t. butter, softened

salt and pepper to taste
2 English muffins, split and
   toasted

Cover eggs with water in a small saucepan over high heat. Bring to a boil; cook 15 minutes. While eggs are still warm, peel and chop; place in a bowl. Stir in vinegar, butter, salt and pepper. Spoon onto English muffins. Makes 2 servings.

Kimberly Wines
Front Royal, VA

Garden-Fresh Frittata

Pick vegetables fresh from your garden for this delicious meal.

3 egg whites
1 egg
2 T. fresh chives, chopped
⅛ t. salt
⅛ t. pepper
½ c. redskin potatoes, cubed
½ c. broccoli flowerets

¼ c. yellow pepper, chopped
⅓ c. water
½ c. canola oil
Garnish: chopped fresh chives,
   diced tomatoes, shredded
   Cheddar cheese

Beat together egg whites, egg, chives, salt and pepper in a bowl until thoroughly combined; set aside. Add potatoes to a lightly greased oven-proof skillet over medium heat; sauté 5 to 6 minutes, until browned. Add broccoli, yellow pepper and water; cover skillet with lid. Cook 3 minutes, or until potatoes are tender; remove lid and allow liquid to evaporate. Add oil to skillet, thoroughly coating all vegetables. Pour egg mixture over vegetables; allow to set slightly, then stir. Cover skillet and cook frittata 3 minutes, or until eggs are set but not dry. Remove lid from skillet and place skillet under broiler, allowing top of frittata to brown. Garnish as desired. Serves 4.

Spinach and Mozzarella Quiche

"One of my friends from church insists on having a piece of this quiche whenever I make it…it's quick, easy and delicious!"

5-oz. pkg. baby spinach
2 T. water
9-inch deep-dish pie crust
1 c. shredded mozzarella
  cheese
3 eggs, beaten

½ c. sour cream
½ c. half-and-half
nutmeg, salt and pepper to
  taste
Garnish: grape tomatoes,
  halved

In a saucepan over medium heat, steam spinach in water 2 minutes. Drain well; press moisture out of spinach and sprinkle spinach over pie crust. Sprinkle cheese evenly over spinach. Whisk together remaining ingredients except garnish in a bowl; pour over cheese. Bake at 325 degrees for 50 minutes. Let cool 10 minutes before cutting. Garnish with tomatoes. Makes 6 servings.

Patricia Smith
Tehachapi, CA

just for you

Bake a quiche in muffin or custard cups for oh-so-simple individual servings. When making minis, reduce the baking time by about 10 minutes and check for doneness with a toothpick.

Ham + Gruyère Egg Cups

"This recipe is always on our Sunday brunch table. It is quick, easy and tasty...very pretty too!"

—Sonya

12 thin slices deli ham
¾ c. shredded Gruyère
   cheese
1 doz. eggs
salt and pepper to taste
¾ c. half-and-half
2 T. grated Parmesan cheese
Garnish: pepper

Spray 12 muffin cups or ramekins with non-stick vegetable spray. Line each muffin cup or ramekin with a slice of ham folded in half. Top each ham slice with one tablespoon Gruyère cheese, an egg cracked into the cup, a sprinkle of salt and pepper, one tablespoon half-and-half and ½ teaspoon Parmesan cheese. Place muffin tin or ramekins on a baking sheet. Bake at 450 degrees for 15 minutes, or until eggs are set. If using a muffin tin, allow baked eggs to cool several minutes before removing them from the muffin tin. Cool slightly before serving in ramekins. Sprinkle with pepper. Makes one dozen.

Sonya Labbe
Santa Monica, CA

Ham and Potato Casserole

4 potatoes, peeled and cubed
1 lb. cooked ham, cubed
½ c. onion, chopped
10¾-oz. can cream of
   mushroom or cream of
   chicken soup

1¼ c. milk
1½ c. favorite shredded
   cheese, divided
salt and pepper to taste

Place potatoes in a saucepan filled with boiling salted water; cook over medium-high heat until almost tender, about 12 to 15 minutes. Drain and place in a lightly greased 13"x9" baking pan. Sprinkle ham and onion on top of potato mixture. Mix together soup, milk and one cup cheese in a bowl; pour over top of potatoes. Sprinkle with remaining cheese. Bake, uncovered, at 350 degrees for 25 minutes, or until hot and bubbly. At serving time, season with salt and pepper to taste. Serves 4.

Linda Ervin
Durant, OK

Warm Country Gingerbread Waffles

Serve with brown sugar, powdered sugar, hot maple syrup or raspberries.

2 c. all-purpose flour
1 t. cinnamon
½ t. ground ginger
½ t. salt
1 c. molasses

½ c. butter
1½ t. baking soda
1 c. buttermilk
1 egg, beaten

Combine flour, cinnamon, ginger and salt. Heat molasses and butter in a saucepan until butter melts. Remove from heat and stir in baking soda. Add buttermilk and egg; fold in flour mixture. Cook in a preheated greased waffle iron according to manufacturer's instructions. Makes nine 4-inch waffles.

Sausage Bean
Gumbo, page 143

quick + easy favorites

It's 5:00. Do you know what's for supper? Of course you do! Delicious supper solutions are at your fingertips...making weeknights a breeze. From the comforts of Tamale Pie to crowd-pleasing Lasagna Rolls to kid-friendly Cheeseburger & Fries Casserole, these recipes get you in and out of the kitchen *fast!*

Mary's Broiled Steak Tips

1 to 2 lbs. beef steak tips
1 to 2 8-oz. bottles Italian salad
   dressing
2 tomatoes, diced
1 green pepper, chopped
1 onion, chopped

Optional: zucchini, yellow
   squash or other favorite
   vegetables, cut up
garlic powder, salt and pepper
   to taste
mashed potatoes or rice pilaf

In a large dish, cover steak tips with salad dressing. Cover and refrigerate overnight to marinate; drain and discard dressing. Place steak tips on an ungreased broiler pan along with tomatoes, green pepper, onion and any other desired vegetables. Season with garlic powder, salt and pepper. Broil to desired doneness, turning occasionally, about 5 to 8 minutes per side. Serve with mashed potatoes or rice pilaf. Makes 4 to 6 servings.

Beth McCarthy
Nashua, NH

Pot Roast + Veggies

Prep time is just a few minutes!

make-ahead magic

This pot roast can be made ahead and frozen for up to a month. Wrap it tightly in aluminum foil and store in a plastic zipping bag.

3- to 4-lb. pot roast
4 potatoes, chopped
6 carrots, chopped
1 onion, chopped

10¾-oz. can cream of
   mushroom soup
1½-oz. pkg. onion soup mix
2 T. water

Line a 13"x9" baking pan with aluminum foil; place roast in pan. Arrange vegetables around roast. In a medium mixing bowl, combine mushroom soup and onion soup mix; pour over roast and sprinkle with water. Cover with an additional piece of aluminum foil. Bake at 300 degrees for 4 hours. Makes 6 to 8 servings.

Michelle Thornton
Surry, NH

Texas Steak Sandwiches
Julie Horn (Chrisney, IN)

8 slices frozen Texas toast
1½ lbs. deli roast beef, sliced
steak sauce to taste

16 slices provolone cheese
Optional: sautéed green pepper
and red onion slices

Place Texas toast on an ungreased baking sheet. Bake at 425 degrees for 5 minutes per side, or until softened and lightly golden; set aside. Warm roast beef in a skillet over medium heat until most of juice has evaporated; stir in steak sauce. Place one cheese slice on each toast slice. Divide beef evenly among toast slices; top with remaining 8 cheese slices and, if desired, sautéed green pepper and onion slices. Place beef-topped toast on an ungreased baking sheet; bake at 425 degrees until cheese melts. Makes 8 open-faced sandwiches.

Spanish Rice and Beef

This recipe is perfect when you need to get dinner on the table in a hurry, after working all day and shuttling the kids to their after-school activities. Warm up some dinner rolls...dinner is served!

1 lb. ground beef
14½-oz. can stewed tomatoes, undrained
10-oz. pkg. frozen corn or mixed vegetables
1 c. water

½ t. salt
½ t. dried oregano
½ t. chili powder
¼ t. garlic powder
⅛ t. pepper
1½ c. instant rice, uncooked

Brown ground beef in a large skillet over medium heat; drain. Add tomatoes, frozen corn or vegetables, water and seasonings. Bring to a boil; boil about 2 minutes, or until vegetables are tender. Stir in uncooked rice. Cover; remove from heat and let stand about 5 minutes. Fluff rice with a fork before serving. Makes 4 to 6 servings.

Sue Hogarth
Lancaster, CA

Beefy Hashbrown Bake

4 c. frozen shredded
  hashbrowns
3 T. vegetable oil
⅛ t. pepper
1 lb. ground beef
1 c. water
0.87-oz. pkg. brown gravy mix

½ t. garlic salt
2 c. frozen mixed vegetables
2.8-oz. can French-fried
  onions, divided
1 c. shredded Cheddar cheese,
  divided

"A tasty meal-in-a-pan that my family and I really enjoy."

—Sue

In a bowl, combine frozen hashbrowns, oil and pepper. Press into a greased 8"x8" baking pan. Bake, uncovered, at 350 degrees for 15 to 20 minutes, until hashbrowns are thawed and set. Meanwhile, brown ground beef in a skillet over medium heat; drain. Add water, gravy mix and garlic salt to beef in skillet. Bring to a boil; cook and stir 2 minutes. Add frozen vegetables; cook and stir 5 minutes. Stir in half of the onions and ½ cup cheese. Pour beef mixture over hashbrowns. Bake, uncovered, at 350 degrees for 5 to 10 minutes. Sprinkle with remaining onions and cheese; bake 5 minutes longer, or until cheese melts. Makes 4 servings.

Sue Klapper
Muskego, WI

Shepherd's Pie   Dale Evans (Frankfort, MI)

"My daughters are both married teachers, so this is the perfect quick & easy recipe...and their husbands love it!"

2 lbs. ground beef
1 onion, diced
6-oz. pkg. frozen corn, thawed
10¾-oz. can cream of mushroom
   soup

4 c. instant mashed potatoes,
   cooked
Garnish: chopped fresh parsley

In a large skillet, brown ground beef over medium-high heat; drain and add onion and corn. Thoroughly blend in soup, and warm through. Serve over mashed potatoes. Garnish with parsley. Makes 8 servings.

Country Bean Casserole

The brown sugar gives this dish a subtle, sweet flavor that's so good.

½ lb. ground beef
½ lb. bacon, chopped
1 c. onion, chopped
16-oz. can pork & beans
15½-oz. can lima beans, drained
16-oz. can kidney beans, drained

½ c. catsup
½ c. brown sugar, packed
1 T. mustard
1 t. salt
2 t. vinegar

Brown ground beef, bacon and onion in a large skillet over medium to medium-high heat; drain. Add remaining ingredients, stirring well. Pour into an ungreased 2½-quart casserole dish. Bake, covered, at 350 degrees for 40 to 45 minutes, until bubbly. Makes 8 to 10 servings.

Leona Toland
Baltimore, MD

Sour Cream Noodles

Easy, fast and economical…sure to be a family pleaser.

1 lb. ground beef
26-oz. jar spaghetti sauce
8-oz. pkg. elbow macaroni, uncooked

8 oz. sour cream

Brown ground beef in a large skillet over medium heat; drain. Add spaghetti sauce. Spread macaroni in a single layer over beef and sauce; cover. Cook over medium heat 10 minutes, or until noodles are tender; add water as necessary to prevent sticking. Add sour cream and mix; heat through. Makes 4 to 6 servings.

Leslie House
Middlebury, CT

take-along tips

This recipe comes together in a hurry and can travel well. Simply prepare it completely and store it in an airtight container. Reheat it on the stovetop, if needed, before serving.

Hamburger Stroganoff

1½ lbs. ground beef
1 onion, chopped
1 to 2 t. garlic, minced
10¾-oz. can cream of mushroom soup
10¾-oz. can cream of chicken soup
1½ c. sour cream
pepper to taste
16-oz. pkg. sliced mushrooms
2 T. butter
cooked wide egg noodles
Garnish: shredded Parmesan cheese

Brown ground beef in a large skillet over medium heat; drain. Add onion and garlic; cook until onion is translucent. Stir in soups; reduce heat and simmer 10 to 15 minutes. Stir in sour cream and pepper; simmer an additional 5 minutes. Meanwhile, in a separate skillet over medium heat, sauté mushrooms in butter until tender, about 3 to 4 minutes. Serve beef mixture and mushrooms over cooked noodles. Garnish with cheese. Makes 6 servings.

Tina Wright
White House, TN

Stuffed Shells

2 lbs. ground beef
3 cloves garlic, minced
Italian seasoning to taste
salt and pepper to taste
2 24-oz. jars spaghetti sauce
1 c. shredded mozzarella cheese, divided
12-oz. pkg. jumbo pasta shells, cooked and drained

Brown ground beef with garlic, Italian seasoning, salt and pepper in a large skillet over medium-high heat; drain. Stir in ½ jar spaghetti sauce and ½ cup cheese; spoon into shells. Pour ½ jar spaghetti sauce into the bottom of an ungreased 13"x9" baking pan or 6 to 8 gratin dishes; add shells. Pour remaining spaghetti sauce over shells; sprinkle with remaining cheese. Bake, uncovered, at 350 degrees for 30 to 40 minutes. Serves 6 to 8.

Melle Bain
Waco, TX

Cheeseburger & Fries Casserole

Shari Miller (Hobart, IN)

2 lbs. ground beef, browned and
   drained
10¾-oz. can golden mushroom
   soup
10¾-oz. can Cheddar cheese soup

16-oz. pkg. frozen crinkle-cut
   French fries
Garnish: chopped tomato, chopped
   dill pickle

Combine ground beef and soups in a large bowl; spread in a greased 13"x9" baking pan. Arrange French fries on top. Bake, uncovered, at 350 degrees for 50 to 55 minutes, until fries are golden. Serve topped with tomato and pickle. Makes 6 to 8 servings.

Beefy Chow Mein Noodle Casserole

2 lbs. ground beef
1 onion, chopped
10¾-oz. can cream of celery
  soup
10¾-oz. can golden mushroom
  soup
1¼ c. water

1 c. instant rice, uncooked
1 T. Worcestershire sauce
1 t. garlic powder
½ t. salt
5-oz. can chow mein noodles
Garnish: chopped fresh parsley

Brown ground beef and onion in a large skillet over medium heat; drain. Stir together soups and remaining ingredients except noodles in a large bowl. Add to beef mixture; mix well. Pour into a lightly greased 13"x9" baking pan. Bake, uncovered, at 375 degrees for 20 minutes, or until bubbly. Sprinkle with chow mein noodles. Bake, uncovered, an additional 5 to 10 minutes. Garnish with parsley. Serves 16.

Vicki Cox
Bland, MO

favorite recipes

Copy tried & true recipes onto file cards and have them laminated at a copying store. Punch a hole in the upper left corner and thread cards onto a key ring...now you can hang them on the fridge and they'll always be handy.

Mexican Lasagna

Lasagna adopts a Mexican flavor in this recipe. Corn tortillas take the place of lasagna noodles; Cheddar and Monterey Jack cheese replace mozzarella; and jalapeño, cumin, cilantro and avocado give it its south-of-the-border flavor.

½ lb. mild ground pork sausage
½ lb. ground beef
1 jalapeño pepper, seeded and finely chopped
⅔ c. canned diced tomatoes with green chiles
1 t. garlic powder
1 t. ground cumin
½ t. salt
½ t. pepper
10¾-oz. can cream of celery soup

10¾-oz. can cream of mushroom soup
10-oz. can enchilada sauce
18 6-inch corn tortillas, divided
2 c. shredded Cheddar cheese, divided
1 c. shredded Monterey Jack cheese
1 tomato, seeded and diced
4 green onions, chopped
¼ c. fresh cilantro, chopped
Optional: 1 avocado, chopped

Cook sausage and ground beef in a skillet over medium-high heat, stirring until meat crumbles and is no longer pink. Drain. Stir in jalapeño and next 5 ingredients; cook until thoroughly heated. Stir together soups and enchilada sauce in a saucepan; cook over medium-high heat until thoroughly heated. Spoon one-third of sauce onto bottom of a lightly greased 13"x9" baking pan; top with 6 tortillas. Spoon half of beef mixture and one-third of sauce over tortillas; sprinkle with half of Cheddar cheese. Top with 6 tortillas; repeat layers, ending with tortillas. Sprinkle with Monterey Jack cheese and next 3 ingredients. Bake, uncovered, at 350 degrees for 30 minutes. Top with avocado, if desired. Serves 6 to 8.

Tamale Pie

Ready-made tamales make this pie oh-so quick.

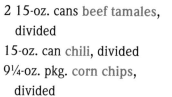

2 15-oz. cans beef tamales, divided
15-oz. can chili, divided
9¼-oz. pkg. corn chips, divided
1 onion, minced and divided
2 c. shredded Cheddar cheese, divided

Chop one can of tamales; set aside. Spread one cup chili in the bottom of a greased 2-quart casserole dish; layer half the corn chips, half the onion and chopped tamales on top. Sprinkle with half the cheese; repeat layers, ending with whole tamales topped with cheese. Cover and bake at 350 degrees for one hour. Let stand 10 minutes before serving. Serves 12.

Kelly Cook
Dunedin, FL

take-along tips

This makes enough for a crowd, so it's perfect to take to a church supper or family reunion. Bake the pie completely, then wrap tightly in aluminum foil and place in a casserole tote to take it to your gathering.

Mile-High Pork Chop Casserole

Use red or yellow peppers for color and variety.

4 boneless pork chops
salt and pepper to taste
2 T. vegetable oil
1 c. long-cooking rice, uncooked
1 tomato, sliced
1 green pepper, sliced
1 onion, sliced
10-oz. can beef consommé
Garnish: fresh parsley, chopped

Sprinkle pork chops on both sides with salt and pepper. Heat oil in a skillet over medium heat; cook chops on both sides until golden. Set aside. Sprinkle rice in a lightly greased 11"x7" baking pan. Arrange pork chops on top of rice. Place tomato, green pepper and onion slices on top of each pork chop. Pour consommé over all; cover. Bake at 350 degrees for 1½ hours, or until pork chops are tender and rice has absorbed all the liquid. Sprinkle with parsley. Makes 4 servings.

Karen Shepherd
Elko, NV

Stir-Fried Pork & Noodles

5 c. water, divided
2 3-oz. pkgs. Oriental ramen
   noodles with seasoning
   packet, divided
2 t. vegetable oil, divided
16-oz. pkg. frozen stir-fry
   vegetables, thawed

½ c. onion, sliced
3 cloves garlic, minced
¾ lb. boneless pork chops,
   cut into strips
1 T. cornstarch
Optional: soy sauce

In a saucepan over high heat, bring 4 cups water to a boil. Add noodles; set aside seasoning packets. Boil noodles 3 minutes; drain. Meanwhile, add one teaspoon oil to a large skillet over medium-high heat. Add vegetables, onion and garlic to skillet. Cook and stir until crisp-tender, about 4 minutes. Set vegetable mixture aside in a bowl. Add pork and remaining oil to skillet. Cook and stir just until pork is cooked through. Remove pork to bowl with vegetables. Combine remaining water, reserved seasoning packets and cornstarch in skillet. Stir until simmering and well blended. Cook one minute, or until slightly thickened. Add noodles; toss to coat. Add pork and vegetables. Cook and stir gently over low heat until warmed through. Serve with soy sauce, if desired. Makes 4 servings.

Jill Ross
Pickerington, OH

"Stir-fries are my easy answer to dinner in a hurry. They're so adaptable too...you can use boneless chicken, beef or even portabella mushrooms instead of pork."
—Jill

Sausage & Spanish Rice Skillet

"My husband and I came up with this tasty recipe. My daughters and grandchildren really enjoy it!"

—Kathy

1 lb. smoked pork sausage links, cut into one-inch thick pieces
2 to 3 t. vegetable oil

1½ c. instant rice, uncooked
1½ c. chicken broth
8-oz. jar mild or hot salsa
2 c. shredded Cheddar cheese

In a large skillet over medium-high heat, brown sausage in oil; drain. Meanwhile, prepare rice according to package directions, using broth instead of water. Add rice and salsa to sausage in skillet; sprinkle with cheese. Cover and cook over low heat a few minutes, until cheese melts. Makes 4 servings.

Kathy Smith
Cincinnati, OH

Cajun Skillet Rice

"I adapted this hearty recipe from one that my mom gave me."

—Janine

1 T. olive oil
1 c. onion, chopped
1 c. green pepper, chopped
1 c. red pepper, chopped
1 lb. Kielbasa sausage, sliced
2 t. Cajun seasoning
Optional: ⅛ t. cayenne pepper

14½-oz. can fire-roasted or plain diced tomatoes, undrained
1½ c. chicken broth
¾ c. long-cooking rice, uncooked

Heat oil in a large skillet over medium-high heat. Add onions, peppers and sausage; sprinkle with desired seasonings. Sauté until onion is translucent, peppers have softened and sausage is lightly golden. Add tomatoes, broth and uncooked rice. Bring to a fast simmer; turn heat to medium-low and cover. Cook 20 minutes, or until all liquid is absorbed and rice is tender. Serves 4.

Janine Tinklenberg
Redford, MI

Deep-Dish Skillet Pizza

1 loaf frozen bread dough,
  thawed
1 to 2 15-oz. jars pizza sauce
½ lb. ground pork sausage,
  browned and drained
5-oz. pkg. sliced pepperoni

½ c. sliced mushrooms
½ c. green pepper, sliced
Italian seasoning to taste
1 c. shredded mozzarella
  cheese
1 c. shredded Cheddar cheese

Generously grease a large cast-iron skillet. Press thawed dough into the
bottom and up the sides of the skillet. Spread desired amount of pizza
sauce over dough. Add favorite toppings, ending with cheese on top.
Bake at 425 degrees for 30 minutes. Carefully remove skillet from oven.
Let stand several minutes; pizza will finish baking in the skillet. Cut into
wedges to serve. Serves 4.

"This recipe is my husband's. He made us one of these pizzas for supper and now it's the only pizza we ever want to eat. Delicious!"

—Linda

Linda Kilgore
Kittanning, PA

Mama's Mucho Nachos

This may sound like an appetizer, but it's really a meal in itself! Add a crisp green salad and some fresh fruit for a dinner the whole family will love.

7-oz. pkg. tortilla chips
3 c. shredded Colby Jack
  cheese, divided
15½-oz. can fat-free refried
  beans
1 c. chunky salsa or picante
  sauce

1 lb. ground pork sausage,
  browned and drained
1 bunch green onions,
  chopped
1 to 2 tomatoes, chopped
Garnish: sour cream, sliced
  jalapeño peppers

In a greased 3-quart casserole dish, place a layer of tortilla chips. Top with 1½ cups cheese, refried beans and salsa or sauce. Sprinkle with sausage and remaining cheese. Bake, uncovered, at 350 degrees for 10 to 20 minutes, until heated through and cheese is melted. Remove from oven. Top with onions and tomatoes; add sour cream and jalapeño peppers, as desired. Serves 4 to 6.

Janie Branstetter
Duncan, OK

Sausage Bean Gumbo
Jo Cline (Smithville, MO)

Quick & easy...ready in 30 minutes!

14-oz. smoked pork sausage link, sliced

3 15½-oz. cans Great Northern beans, undrained

14½-oz. can diced tomatoes with sweet onions, undrained

1 stalk celery, diced

½ c. green pepper, diced

½ t. garlic powder

¼ t. pepper

Garnish: fresh cilantro, chopped

In a large saucepan over low heat, combine all ingredients except garnish. Cover and simmer about 30 minutes, stirring occasionally. Sprinkle servings with cilantro, if desired. Makes 4 servings.

Hearty Pierogie Casserole

2 to 3 16.9-oz. pkgs. frozen
    favorite-flavor pierogies
1½ to 2 lbs. smoked pork
    sausage, sliced into bite-size
    pieces

26-oz. can cream of
    mushroom soup
3¼ c. milk
2 to 3 c. shredded Cheddar
    cheese

Bring a large saucepan of water to a boil; add pierogies and sausage.
Cook 5 to 7 minutes, until pierogies float; drain. Arrange pierogies and
sausage in a lightly greased 13"x9" glass baking pan. Blend soup and milk
in a bowl; pour over top of pierogie mixture. Top with cheese. Bake,
uncovered, at 350 degrees for 30 to 35 minutes, until soup mixture is
bubbly and cheese is lightly golden. Let stand 5 minutes before serving.
Serves 8.

Sheryl Maksymoski
Grand Rapids, MI

quick side

A crisp green salad goes with all kinds of comforting main
dishes. For a zippy lemon dressing, shake up ½ cup olive
oil, ⅓ cup fresh lemon juice and a tablespoon of Dijon
mustard in a small jar and chill to blend.

Ham & Swiss Casserole

Set a basket of warm rolls and glasses of cold milk on the table...your family will come even before you call them!

8 oz. sour cream
12-oz. pkg. shredded Swiss
  cheese, divided

8-oz. pkg. macaroni, cooked
3 c. cooked ham, chopped

In a small mixing bowl, combine sour cream and three-fourths of cheese. In a lightly greased 13"x9" baking pan, place macaroni and ham. Add sour cream mixture to baking pan; stir until blended. Top with remaining cheese. Bake, uncovered, at 350 degrees for 30 minutes, or until bubbly. Makes 6 to 8 servings.

Lauren Klein
Savannah, GA

simple swap

Use shredded Cheddar or Gruyére cheese in place of the Swiss cheese in this dish if your crowd would prefer something with a different flavor.

Dressed-Up Dogs

8 hot dogs
8 slices rye bread, toasted
mayonnaise-type salad
   dressing to taste

2 kosher dill pickles, each cut
   lengthwise into 4 slices
4 slices Swiss cheese
Optional: mustard to taste

Slice hot dogs lengthwise, taking care not to cut all the way through. Place hot dogs cut-side down on a lightly greased hot griddle. Cook on each side until golden and heated through; set aside. Spread 4 slices bread with salad dressing; top each with 2 pickle slices, 2 hot dogs and one slice cheese. Spread remaining 4 slices bread with mustard, if using. Place on top of sandwiches. Makes 4 sandwiches.

Shawna Weathers
Judsonia, AR

Smoky Sausage Skillet

"One of my favorite go-to quick meals...it practically cooks itself!"

—Carla

14-oz. pkg. mini smoked
   turkey sausages
10-oz. pkg. sliced mushrooms
2 t. garlic, chopped

2 14½-oz. cans cut green
   beans, drained
Optional: cooked rice

Spray a large skillet with non-stick vegetable spray. Brown sausages over medium heat; add mushrooms and garlic. Cook, stirring occasionally, until mushrooms are tender. Add green beans; cook over low heat until heated through. Serve over cooked rice, if desired. Serves 6.

Carla Langston
Las Vegas, NV

Corn & Bacon Chowder

For added texture, stir in ½ cup frozen corn kernels and then sprinkle with an extra slice of crisp, chopped bacon to finish. The contrast of sweet corn and smoky bacon makes this delicious comfort food.

8 slices bacon, diced
1 c. onion, chopped
4 14.5-oz. cans chicken broth
4 c. potatoes, peeled and diced

4 c. creamed corn
salt and pepper to taste
Garnish: chopped fresh parsley

Cook bacon in a Dutch oven over medium heat until almost crisp; add onion and cook until tender. Add broth, potatoes and corn; cover and bring to a boil. Reduce heat; simmer 12 to 15 minutes, until potatoes are tender. Add salt and pepper to taste; garnish with parsley. Serves 8.

Judy Voster
Neenah, WI

Polynesian Chicken

Baked chicken pieces combine with pineapple and orange soy sauce…a delicious taste of the islands!

2 lbs. chicken, cut up
8¼-oz. can pineapple chunks, drained and juice reserved
½ c. orange juice
¼ c. soy sauce
3 T. brown sugar, packed
2 T. dried, minced onion
1 t. ground ginger
¼ t. pepper
¼ c. water
2 t. cornstarch
11-oz. can mandarin oranges, drained
4 c. hot cooked rice

Arrange chicken pieces in a single layer in an ungreased 13"x9" baking pan; set aside. In a bowl, combine reserved pineapple juice, orange juice, soy sauce, brown sugar, onion, ginger and pepper; pour over chicken. Cover and refrigerate one hour or overnight, turning once. Bake, covered, at 350 degrees for 30 minutes, or until tender. Uncover and bake 20 to 25 more minutes, until golden and juices run clear when chicken is pierced with a fork. Remove chicken from baking pan; keep warm on a platter. Skim off fat from pan drippings. Combine water and cornstarch with pan juices in a medium saucepan; heat until thickened and bubbly. Stir in pineapple and oranges and warm through; pour over chicken. Serve with cooked rice. Serves 8.

Norma Burton
Meridian, ID

Deb's Chicken Florentine

16-oz. pkg. linguine pasta,
  uncooked
2 T. olive oil
3 cloves garlic, minced
4 boneless, skinless chicken
  breasts, thinly sliced
1¼ c. fat-free zesty Italian
  salad dressing, divided

8 sun-dried tomatoes, chopped
8-oz. pkg. sliced mushrooms
5-oz. pkg. baby spinach
cracked pepper to taste
Optional: grated Parmesan
  cheese

Cook pasta according to package directions; drain. While pasta is
cooking, warm oil in a skillet over medium heat. Add garlic and cook
2 minutes. Add chicken; cook until no longer pink. Drizzle chicken with
one cup salad dressing. Stir in tomatoes and mushrooms; cover skillet and
simmer until mushrooms are softened. Add spinach; cover skillet again.
Cook another 2 to 3 minutes, just until spinach is wilted; stir and sprinkle
with pepper. Toss cooked linguine with remaining salad dressing. Serve
chicken and vegetables over linguine; garnish as desired. Makes 6 servings.

Deb Eaton
Mesa, AZ

"My husband loves Italian food! When a local restaurant closed, he was sad that he couldn't get his favorite dish anymore, so I recreated it for him at home. You can substitute frozen spinach, canned mushrooms or leftover rotisserie chicken."

—Deb

Spicy Chicken Casserole

A hearty, creamy dinner in one dish...with just four ingredients!

4 to 5 boneless, skinless chicken breasts

2 10¾-oz. cans cream of chicken soup

2 10¾-oz. cans nacho cheese soup

3 to 4 c. tortilla chips, crushed and divided

Cover chicken breasts with water in a large saucepan. Simmer over medium-high heat just until cooked through. Drain, saving broth for another use. Cool chicken slightly; shred into bite-size pieces and set aside. Combine soups in a saucepan. Stir well; cook over medium heat until bubbly. Remove from heat. In a greased 13"x9" baking pan, layer half of chopped chicken, half of soup mixture and half of the crushed chips. Repeat layers. Cover and bake at 350 degrees for 20 minutes, or until heated through. Serves 6.

Martha Stephens
Sibley, LA

Ranch Chicken Wraps

½ t. vegetable oil

4 boneless, skinless chicken breasts, cut into strips

2.8-oz. can French-fried onions

¼ c. bacon bits

8-oz. pkg. shredded Cheddar cheese

lettuce leaves

8 to 10 8-inch flour tortillas

ranch salad dressing

Heat oil in a large non-stick skillet over medium heat. Add chicken and cook until chicken is golden and juices run clear when chicken is pierced. Add onions, bacon bits and cheese to skillet; cook until cheese melts. Place several lettuce leaves on each tortilla and spoon chicken mixture down center; roll up. Serve with ranch salad dressing. Makes 8 to 10 wraps.

Lea Ann Burwell
Charles Town, WV

Zesty Picante Chicken

Spice up suppertime with yummy southwestern-style chicken breasts…made in the slow cooker!

4 boneless, skinless chicken breasts
16-oz. jar picante sauce
16-oz. can black beans, drained and rinsed

4 slices American cheese
2¼ c. cooked rice
Optional: chopped green onions

Place chicken in a 5-quart slow cooker; add picante sauce. Spread black beans over the top. Cover and cook on high setting for 3 hours, or until juices run clear when chicken is pierced with a fork. Top with cheese slices; cover and heat until melted. Spoon over rice to serve. Garnish with green onions, if desired. Serves 4.

Sonya Collet
Sioux City, IA

Chicken and Spinach Calzones

A great recipe using prepared dough…what a time-saver!

2 boneless, skinless chicken
  breasts, cubed
¼ c. onion, chopped
1 c. frozen chopped spinach,
  cooked and drained
2 t. dried basil

¾ c. pizza sauce
½ c. ricotta cheese
3 oz. mozzarella cheese,
  cubed
11-oz. can refrigerated pizza
  dough

Sauté chicken in a large skillet over medium-high heat until juices run clear when chicken is pierced with a fork; add onion and sauté 2 minutes. Reduce heat; add spinach, basil, pizza sauce and ricotta cheese. Remove from heat; stir in mozzarella cheese and set aside. Divide pizza dough into 4 equal pieces; roll each piece into a 6-inch circle. Divide chicken mixture among dough circles; fold dough in half. Seal edges with a fork; set on a lightly greased baking sheet. Bake at 425 degrees for 15 minutes, or until crust is golden brown. Makes 4 servings.

Jennifer Smith
Manchester, CT

make-ahead magic

Let the calzones cool completely after baking. Wrap them tightly in aluminum foil and store them in an airtight container. Place them in the freezer for up to one month.

perfect timing

When whipping up a speedy supper, use a kitchen timer… let it watch the clock so that you don't have to.

Mini Chicken Pot Pies

This is a speedy meal for a busy night. Just add some mashed potatoes, a vegetable on the side and a simple dessert.

7½-oz. tube refrigerated
  biscuits
1 c. cooked chicken, diced
10¾-oz. can cream of chicken
  soup

⅔ c. shredded sharp Cheddar
  cheese
salt and pepper to taste

Spray 8 to 10 muffin cups with non-stick vegetable spray. Place a biscuit in each muffin cup; press in bottom and one-fourth of the way up the sides. In a bowl, combine remaining ingredients; stir until well blended. Spoon chicken mixture into biscuit cups, filling about three-fourths full. Bake at 350 degrees for 10 to 15 minutes, until biscuits are golden. Makes 4 to 5 servings, 2 pot pies each.

Amy Hunt
Traphill, NC

Jackie's Quick Stir-Fry

"This is my version of a speedy stir-fry. Sometimes I use two kinds of meat or any extra veggies I have in the fridge for a tasty new meal made with leftovers."

—Jackie

16-oz. pkg. shredded
  broccoli-carrot mix
¼ c. vegetable oil, divided
1 c. cooked ham, pork, chicken
  or shrimp, chopped or sliced
3 T. rice vinegar
3 T. soy sauce

3 T. sugar
salt and pepper to taste
3-oz. pkg. chicken ramen
  noodles with seasoning
  packet
2-oz. pkg. slivered almonds
3 T. sesame seed

In a large skillet over medium-high heat, cook and stir shredded vegetables in 2 tablespoons oil. Add meat to skillet. In a small bowl, mix remaining oil, vinegar, soy sauce, sugar, salt, pepper and seasoning packet from ramen noodle package. Add oil mixture to skillet; stir well. Add almonds and sesame seed. Crush ramen noodles and add to skillet; simmer until noodles are soft, 3 to 4 minutes. Makes 4 servings.

Jackie Antweiler
Evergreen, CO

Chicken-Cashew Casserole

2 10¾-oz. cans cream of
  mushroom soup
2 c. cooked chicken, diced
1 c. celery, diced
⅔ c. water
½ c. onion, grated
8½-oz. container cashews

8-oz. can sliced water chestnuts,
  drained and coarsely chopped
8-oz. pkg. sliced mushrooms
1 cup buttery crackers,
  crushed
2 T. butter, melted
Garnish: chopped green onions

Combine all ingredients except crackers and butter in a large bowl.
Spread in a lightly greased 13"x9" baking pan. Bake, uncovered, at
350 degrees for 30 minutes. Mix together crackers and butter in a small
bowl; sprinkle over top of casserole. Bake an additional 10 minutes.
Garnish with green onions. Serves 6.

Doris Wilson
Denver, IA

Mushroom Fried Rice

"My aunt Merle often serves this dish when we're invited for supper at her house...we enjoy it very much!"

–Jamie

2 to 3 t. vegetable oil
1 c. sliced mushrooms
1 onion, chopped
1 c. cooked chicken, turkey or ham, diced
seasoned salt and pepper to taste
2 c. instant rice, uncooked
½ c. peas, corn or mixed vegetables
10½-oz. can beef broth
1¼ c. water
1 t. soy sauce
½ t. dried parsley

In a large skillet, heat oil over medium heat. Add mushrooms, onion, meat, seasoned salt and pepper. Cook, stirring often, until mushrooms and onion are tender. Add uncooked rice and vegetables; cook and stir 2 to 3 minutes. Add remaining ingredients. Reduce heat to low; cover and simmer about 10 minutes, or until rice is tender and liquid is absorbed. Serves 4.

Jamie Courchesne
Alberta, Canada

Lisa's Chicken Tortilla Soup

take-along tips

Once you have prepared the soup, transfer it to a slow cooker. Secure the slow cooker and transport it to your gathering. Simply turn on the slow cooker when you arrive at your destination to keep the soup warm.

4 14½-oz. cans chicken broth
4 10-oz. cans diced tomatoes with green chiles
1 c. canned or frozen corn
30-oz. can refried beans
5 c. cooked chicken, shredded
Garnish: shredded Mexican-blend cheese, corn chips or tortilla strips, chopped fresh cilantro

Combine broth and tomatoes with chiles in a large stockpot over medium heat. Stir in corn and beans; bring to a boil. Reduce heat to low and simmer 5 minutes, stirring frequently. Add chicken and heat through. Garnish bowls of soup as desired. Serves 6 to 8.

Lisa Johnson
Hallsville, TX

Lisa's Chicken
Tortilla Soup

Oodles of Noodles Casserole

To toast the almonds, just spread them in an ungreased baking pan and bake at 350 degrees for 10 to 15 minutes, stirring occasionally.

8-oz. pkg. medium egg noodles,
   uncooked and divided
2 T. butter
2 T. all-purpose flour
1 t. salt
¼ t. pepper

2 c. milk
1 c. shredded Cheddar cheese
10-oz. pkg. frozen broccoli
   spears, cooked
2 c. cooked turkey, diced
⅓ c. slivered almonds, toasted

Cook half the noodles according to package directions, reserving the rest for another recipe; drain and set aside. Melt butter in a saucepan over low heat; blend in flour, salt and pepper. Stir until smooth and bubbly. Gradually add milk, stirring until thickened. Remove from heat and add cheese; stir until melted. Dice broccoli stems, leaving the flowerets intact. Combine noodles, diced broccoli and turkey in a lightly greased 8"x8" baking pan or ramekins; pour cheese sauce over top. Lightly press flowerets into sauce; sprinkle with almonds. Bake, uncovered, at 350 degrees for 15 minutes. Serves 4.

Beth Kramer
Port Saint Lucie, FL

mistakes made right

Oops! If a simmering pot starts to burn on the bottom, don't worry. Spoon the unburned portion into another pan, being careful not to scrape up the scorched part on the bottom. The burned taste usually won't linger.

Turkey & Broccoli Alfredo

Serve with fresh biscuits for a well-rounded meal.

6-oz. pkg. fettuccine, uncooked
2 c. frozen chopped broccoli
10¾-oz. can cream of
   mushroom soup
½ c. milk
¾ c. grated Parmesan cheese
3 c. cooked turkey, cubed
⅛ t. pepper

Prepare fettuccine according to package directions. Add broccoli in the last 5 minutes of cooking; drain. In a large skillet over medium-high heat, mix soup, milk, cheese, turkey, pepper and fettuccine mixture; cook until heated through, stirring often. Makes 4 servings.

Wendy Jacobs
Idaho Falls, ID

Poor Man's Cordon Bleu

A quick and easy variation on a classic.

16 slices deli turkey
8 slices deli ham
16 slices Swiss cheese
½ c. water
2 c. Italian-flavored dry bread
   crumbs, divided

For each turkey roll, lay out 2 turkey slices, overlapping ends by 2 to 3 inches. Add a ham slice, centered on turkey slices. Place 2 cheese slices on top, with ends barely touching. Roll up, starting on one short side. Repeat with remaining ingredients to make 8 rolls. Dip rolls into water to dampen; coat in bread crumbs, reserving ¼ cup bread crumbs for topping. Place rolls seam-side down in a greased 13"x9" baking pan. Sprinkle reserved crumbs on top. Bake, uncovered, at 350 degrees for 15 to 20 minutes, until lightly golden and cheese is melted. Serves 4.

Linda Lamb
Round Rock, TX

Caesar Focaccia Sandwich

2 c. mixed salad greens
¼ c. Caesar salad dressing
8-inch round focaccia bread or
  round loaf, halved horizontally
4 slices Cheddar cheese
¼ lb. deli ham, thinly shaved

¼ lb. deli turkey, thinly shaved
1 tomato, sliced
1 slice red onion, separated
  into rings
Garnish: pickles, potato chips

Toss salad greens with salad dressing in a small bowl; set aside. Layer the bottom half of focaccia with greens mixture and remaining ingredients except garnish. Add the top half of focaccia; cut into halves or quarters. Serve with pickles and chips on the side. Serves 2 to 4.

Wendy Ball
Battle Creek, MI

Grilled Salmon BLTs

Lemony dill mayonnaise is the secret ingredient in this recipe!

⅓ c. mayonnaise
2 t. fresh dill, chopped
1 t. lemon zest
4 1-inch thick salmon fillets
¼ t. salt
⅛ t. pepper

8 ½-inch thick slices country-style bread
4 romaine lettuce leaves
2 tomatoes, sliced
6 slices bacon, crisply cooked and halved

Stir together mayonnaise, dill and zest in a small bowl; set aside. Sprinkle salmon with salt and pepper; place on a lightly greased hot grill, skin-side down. Cover and cook over medium heat about 10 to 12 minutes, without turning, until cooked through. Slide a thin metal spatula between salmon and skin; lift salmon and transfer to a plate. Discard skin. Arrange bread slices on grill; cook until lightly toasted on both sides. Spread mayonnaise mixture on one side of 4 bread slices. Top each bread slice with one lettuce leaf, 2 tomato slices, 3 half-slices bacon, one salmon fillet and remaining bread slice. Makes 4 sandwiches.

Edie DeSpain
Logan, UT

Friday Night Sandwiches

For the landlubbers in your family, substitute cooked chicken for the crabmeat.

6-oz. can crabmeat
2 stalks celery, finely chopped
2 green onions, finely chopped
4-oz. can sliced mushrooms,
    drained
1 t. caraway seed

1½ T. mayonnaise
1½ T. sour cream
4 slices bread, toasted
8 slices bacon, crisply cooked
4 slices Swiss cheese

Mix together first 7 ingredients in a bowl; spread over bread slices. Top with bacon and Swiss cheese; heat under broiler until cheese melts. Makes 4 servings.

Cathy Whittemore
Vassalboro, ME

Seafood Fettuccine

Scallops or crab may be substituted for variety.

¾ lb. shrimp, cooked, peeled
    and deveined
4-oz. can mushroom stems and
    pieces, drained
½ t. garlic powder
⅛ t. salt
⅛ t. pepper
¼ c. butter

8-oz. pkg. fettuccine, cooked
    and drained
½ c. grated Parmesan cheese
½ c. milk
½ c. sour cream
Garnish: ½ T. fresh parsley,
    chopped

Sauté shrimp, mushrooms, garlic powder, salt and pepper in butter in a large skillet over medium-high heat 3 to 5 minutes; stir in fettuccine, Parmesan cheese, milk and sour cream. Cook over medium heat until warmed; do not boil. Garnish with parsley. Makes 4 servings.

Lorena Freis
Waterloo, IA

Gingered Shrimp + Snow Peas

A flavorful salad that's a meal in itself!

¾ lb. snow peas, trimmed
1¼ lbs. uncooked medium
   shrimp, cleaned
6 radishes, thinly sliced
4 green onions, thinly sliced
⅓ c. vinegar

1 T. canola oil
1 T. toasted sesame oil
1 T. fresh ginger, peeled and
   grated
salt to taste
2 T. toasted sesame seeds

Place a steamer basket in a large saucepan; fill pan with water and bring to a boil. Add snow peas; cover and cook 2 minutes. Remove basket, reserving boiling water in saucepan; transfer peas to a bowl of ice water to cool. Drain peas and pat dry; cut on the diagonal into ½-inch pieces. Add shrimp directly to boiling water; return to a boil and cook 2 minutes. Drain shrimp; plunge into a bowl of ice water. Drain and pat dry; slice shrimp in half lengthwise. In a large bowl, toss together shrimp, peas, radishes and onions. In a small bowl, whisk together vinegar, oils and ginger; add salt to taste. Drizzle vinegar mixture over salad and top with sesame seeds. Serves 4.

Sandra Sullivan
Aurora, CO

Shrimp Scampi

Shrimp Scampi

2 lbs. uncooked peeled large
   shrimp
½ c. butter
½ c. olive oil
2 T. white wine or lemon juice
¼ c. green onions, minced
¼ c. fresh parsley, minced
1 T. garlic, minced
1 t. salt
pepper to taste
Optional: cooked angel hair
   pasta, lemon wedges

Place shrimp in a large bowl; set aside. In a saucepan over medium-low heat, combine remaining ingredients except pasta and lemon wedges. Cook 3 to 4 minutes, stirring often, until well blended. Pour most of butter mixture over shrimp; toss to coat well. Arrange shrimp in a single layer on a 15"x10" jelly-roll pan. Broil 3 to 4 inches from heat about 5 minutes. Transfer shrimp to a serving platter; drizzle with remaining butter mixture. Serve over angel hair pasta with lemon wedges, if desired. Serves 6.

Vickie
Gooseberry Patch

Virgil's Veggie Fettuccine

2 16-oz. pkgs. fettuccine pasta,
   uncooked
1½ c. half-and-half
2 t. garlic salt or powder
8 c. broccoli, cut into bite-size
   pieces
1 head cauliflower, cut into
   bite-size pieces
8-oz. pkg. sliced mushrooms
salt and pepper to taste
2 to 3 c. grated Parmesan
   cheese

Cook pasta according to package directions; drain. While pasta is cooking, combine half-and-half and garlic salt or powder in an extra-large Dutch oven. Heat over medium heat just until boiling. Add broccoli, cauliflower and mushrooms; stir to moisten. Season with additional garlic salt or powder, if desired, and salt and pepper. Cook over medium heat until vegetables are crisp-tender, stirring frequently; vegetables will cook down. Add cooked pasta; stir until everything is combined and heated through. Gradually add Parmesan cheese; stir until melted. Serve immediately. Makes 8 to 10 servings.

Jodi Spires
Centerville, OH

"My dad knew how to cook only a few things, but they were extraordinary! He has been gone for several years now...when our family sits down to this homemade meal, it's as if he is still right there with us, smiling."

—Jodi

Stuffed Eggplant Boats

2 eggplants, halved lengthwise
1 t. salt
2 potatoes, peeled and chopped
¼ c. olive oil, divided
1 c. onion, diced
1 red pepper, diced
2 cloves garlic, minced
salt and pepper to taste
8-oz. pkg. shredded mozzarella
  cheese
1 c. dry bread crumbs
Garnish: chopped fresh parsley

Scoop out the middle of eggplants to form boats, leaving a 2-inch shell; reserve for another use. Lightly salt boats; spray with non-stick vegetable spray on all sides. Set aside on a greased baking sheet. Cook potatoes in 3 tablespoons olive oil in a skillet over medium heat 5 to 10 minutes, or until golden. Remove with a slotted spoon to a separate plate. Add onion, red pepper and garlic to skillet. Cook until onion is translucent and pepper is tender. Return potatoes to pan; sprinkle with salt and pepper to taste. Fill eggplant boats with mixture. Top with cheese and bread crumbs; drizzle with remaining oil. Bake at 350 degrees for 30 minutes, or until tender. Garnish with fresh parsley. Serve immediately. Serves 4.

Michelle Papp
Rutherford, NJ

no more tears

Place just a corner of a bread slice between your teeth while you're cutting onions and your eyes won't water.

Lasagna Rolls

Double this recipe so you can have one casserole to keep and one to either give away or freeze for holiday company...it freezes for up to one month.

11 lasagna noodles, uncooked
1 lb. Italian sausage, casing removed
1 small onion, chopped
1 clove garlic, minced
26-oz. jar spaghetti sauce
¼ c. dry white wine or chicken broth
3 T. fresh parsley, chopped

½ t. salt
3 c. ricotta cheese
1 c. shredded mozzarella cheese
2 eggs, lightly beaten
⅓ c. fine, dry bread crumbs
2 T. grated Parmesan cheese
1 t. Italian seasoning
½ c. grated Parmesan cheese

Cook lasagna noodles according to package directions; drain. Cut in half crosswise and set aside. Cook sausage, onion and garlic in a large skillet over medium-high heat, stirring until sausage crumbles and is no longer pink; drain. Add spaghetti sauce, wine or broth, parsley and salt, stirring well. Cover and simmer 10 minutes, stirring occasionally. Remove from heat and set aside. Combine ricotta cheese and next 5 ingredients in a bowl, stirring well. Spread ricotta mixture evenly over lasagna noodles. Roll up jelly-roll fashion, starting at narrow end. Place lasagna rolls, seam-side down, in a lightly greased 13"x9" baking pan. Pour meat sauce over rolls and sprinkle with ½ cup Parmesan cheese. Cover and bake at 375 degrees for 30 minutes. Uncover and bake 15 more minutes or until thoroughly heated. Serves 8 to 10.

Tomato Tortellini Soup

Easy and so tasty! Keep the ingredients on hand and you'll be able to stir up a pot of soup in just minutes.

2 cloves garlic, minced
1 T. olive oil
2 14½-oz. cans chicken broth
2 14½-oz. cans diced
   tomatoes, undrained

9-oz. pkg. refrigerated cheese
   tortellini
1 T. fresh basil, chopped, or
   1 t. dried basil
salt and pepper to taste

In a large saucepan over medium heat, cook garlic in oil until fragrant. Stir in broth and tomatoes; bring to a boil. Add tortellini. Reduce heat and simmer about 10 minutes, or until tortellini is tender. Stir in basil; season with salt and pepper. Makes 4 to 6 servings.

Emily Hartzell
Portland, IN

Mexican Egg Bake

Just right served with a side of refried beans.

12 corn tortillas, torn
16-oz. can green chile sauce
16-oz. pkg. shredded Cheddar
   cheese, divided

6 eggs
Garnish: sour cream, shredded
   lettuce, chopped tomato

Layer tortillas, chile sauce and three-fourths of cheese into an ungreased 13"x9" baking pan. Break eggs over top, spacing evenly. Sprinkle with remaining cheese. Bake, uncovered, at 350 degrees for 30 to 40 minutes. Slice into squares and garnish with sour cream, lettuce and tomato. Makes 8 to 10 servings.

Nadine Watson
Aurora, CO

Pasta with Roasted Veggies

Use your family's favorite vegetables to make this dish special!

1 lb. **mixed fresh vegetables**, chopped
salt and **pepper** to taste
2 t. **fresh rosemary**, chopped
2 t. **fresh thyme**, chopped

2 T. **olive oil**
8 oz. **rigatoni**, cooked
2 t. **balsamic vinegar**
2½ T. grated **Parmesan cheese**

Arrange vegetables in a lightly greased 13"x9" baking pan. Season with salt, pepper, rosemary and thyme; pour oil over all and toss. Roast at 500 degrees for 10 minutes, or until browned. Drain vegetables, reserving juice; set aside. In a large serving bowl, toss pasta, vegetables, reserved juice and vinegar. Sprinkle with Parmesan cheese; toss. Makes 4 servings.

Spanish Omelette

This is a great big thick cake of an omelette packed with vegetables and cheese. It can be served warm as a main course, and it tastes just as good cold. You can even take it on a picnic. Serve in hearty wedges with a chunky tomato & onion salad...delicious!

¼ c. olive oil, divided
1 to 2 potatoes, peeled and
    diced
1 onion, sliced
1 red pepper, diced
1 green pepper, diced
1 zucchini, coarsely chopped

⅓ to ½ c. frozen peas
¼ lb. smoked chorizo or
    Kielbasa sausage, diced
5 eggs, lightly beaten
salt and pepper to taste
½ c. shredded Cheddar cheese

Heat 2 tablespoons oil in an oven-proof skillet over high heat. Add potatoes and onion; toss to coat well. Reduce heat to medium-low. Cover and cook 15 minutes, stirring occasionally. Add peppers, zucchini, peas and sausage; mix well. Cover and cook an additional 5 to 8 minutes, until vegetables start to soften. In a large bowl, combine eggs, salt and pepper. Remove skillet from heat; slowly pour vegetable mixture into bowl with eggs. Return empty skillet to stove; add remaining oil and heat over medium-high heat. Pour egg and vegetable mixture into skillet; cook one minute. Reduce heat to low; cook, uncovered, 15 to 20 minutes. Sprinkle omelette with cheese; place under broiler 3 to 5 minutes, until golden and bubbly. Cut into wedges to serve. Makes 4 servings.

Elaine Day
Essex, England

Quick-as-a-Wink Waffles

Laura Strausberger (Roswell, GA)

Try these topped with jam or preserves, syrup or fresh fruit and a dusting of powdered sugar.

2 eggs
¾ c. milk
2 T. vegetable oil
1 c. all-purpose flour

1½ t. baking powder
1½ t. sugar
½ t. salt

Beat eggs in a medium bowl until frothy. Add remaining ingredients; mix until smooth. Pour by ½ cupfuls onto a preheated waffle iron; bake following manufacturer's directions. Serves 4.

Three-Bean Basil
Salad, page 196

scrumptious sides

Stop your side-dish search and start cooking! Make family favorites like Spicy Carrot French Fries or Mom's Squash Casserole. Jazz up the same old standbys with Broccoli Salad of Wonder or Dilled New Potato Salad. These pages are bursting with easy-to-create sides to go with any main dish.

Quick + Easy Parmesan Asparagus

From oven to table in only 15 minutes!

4 lbs. asparagus, trimmed
¼ c. butter, melted
2 c. shredded Parmesan cheese
1 t. salt
½ t. pepper

Place asparagus and one inch of water in a large skillet. Bring to a boil. Reduce heat; cover and simmer 5 to 7 minutes, until crisp-tender. Drain and arrange asparagus in a greased 13"x9" baking pan. Drizzle with butter; sprinkle with Parmesan cheese, salt and pepper. Bake, uncovered, at 350 degrees for 10 to 15 minutes, until cheese is melted. Serves 8 to 10.

Paula Smith
Ottawa, IL

a fresh & healthy alternative

Cutting back on salt? Drizzle steamed vegetables with freshly squeezed lemon juice...you'll never miss the salt!

Bacon-Brown Sugar Brussels Sprouts

A delicious way for your family to enjoy eating this leafy veggie!

4 slices bacon

14-oz. can chicken broth

1 T. brown sugar, packed

1 t. salt

1½ lbs. Brussels sprouts, trimmed and halved

   Cook bacon in a Dutch oven over medium heat 10 minutes, or until crisp. Remove bacon; drain on paper towels, reserving drippings in Dutch oven. Crumble bacon. Add broth, brown sugar and salt to drippings in Dutch oven, and bring to a boil. Stir in Brussels sprouts. Cover and cook 6 to 8 minutes, until tender. Transfer to a serving bowl using a slotted spoon, and sprinkle with bacon. Serve immediately. Serves 6 to 8.

Oh-So-Hot Banana
Peppers

Oh-So-Hot Banana Peppers

18 hot banana peppers
2 lbs. hot ground pork sausage,
  browned and drained
2 6-oz. pkgs. pork-flavored
  stuffing mix, cooked
1 onion, chopped
1 zucchini, chopped
2 eggs, beaten
½ c. brown sugar, packed
16-oz. pkg. shredded Cheddar
  cheese

Slice peppers lengthwise down one side to open up; rinse under running water, removing seeds. Combine sausage and cooked stuffing in a large bowl; add onion and zucchini. Stir in eggs and brown sugar; mix well. Spoon into peppers; arrange peppers in a lightly greased 13"x9" baking pan. Bake, uncovered, at 350 degrees for 1½ hours. Sprinkle with cheese; bake 10 more minutes, or until cheese is melted. Serves 9.

Jean Cerutti
Kittanning, PA

"My friend Sherry brought this to our summer pool party, and it has been my family's favorite ever since. For a milder version, use mild banana peppers and sweet sausage…it's still wonderful!"

—Jean

Kielbasa Bean Pot

So easy to prepare…so flavorful and filling.

2 16-oz. cans pork & beans
1 lb. Kielbasa sausage, sliced
1½-oz. pkg. onion soup mix
⅓ c. catsup
¼ c. water
1 T. mustard
2 t. brown sugar, packed
Garnish: sliced green onions

Combine all ingredients except garnish in an ungreased 2-quart casserole dish. Bake, uncovered, at 350 degrees for one hour. Sprinkle servings with sliced green onions. Serves 6 to 8.

Sharon Crider
Lebanon, MO

Green Bean Supreme

*This isn't your usual green bean casserole. Loaded with cheese and sour cream,
it will be your new favorite!*

1 onion, sliced
1 T. fresh parsley, chopped
3 T. butter, divided
2 T. all-purpose flour
½ t. lemon zest
½ t. salt
⅛ t. pepper

½ c. milk
16-oz. pkg. frozen French-style
   green beans, thawed
8-oz. container sour cream
½ c. shredded Cheddar cheese
¼ c. soft bread crumbs

Cook onion slices and parsley in 2 tablespoons butter in a saucepan over
medium heat until onion is tender, about 5 minutes. Blend in flour, lemon
zest, salt and pepper. Stir in milk; heat until thick and bubbly. Add beans
and sour cream; heat through. Spoon into an ungreased 2-quart casserole
dish; sprinkle with cheese. Melt remaining butter and toss with bread
crumbs in a small bowl; sprinkle over beans. Broil 3 to 4 inches from heat
for 3 minutes, or until golden. Serves 4 to 6.

Spicy Carrot French Fries

The sweet flavor that comes from roasting root vegetables mixed with the spicy seasonings is delicious.

2 lbs. carrots, peeled and cut
    into matchsticks
¼ c. olive oil, divided
1 T. seasoned salt

2 t. ground cumin
1 t. chili powder
1 t. pepper
ranch salad dressing

Place carrots in a large plastic zipping bag. Sprinkle with 3 tablespoons oil and seasonings; toss to coat. Drizzle remaining oil over a baking sheet; place carrots in a single layer on sheet. Bake, uncovered, at 425 degrees for 25 to 35 minutes, until carrots are golden. Serve with salad dressing for dipping. Serves 4 to 6.

Kelly Gray
Weston, WV

take-along tip

Prepare carrots in plastic zipping bag as directed. Take bag of seasoned carrots to your destination and bake on baking sheets before serving.

Marinated Sugar Snap Peas

If you prepare this dish ahead of time, be sure to allow it to come to room temperature before serving.

1½ lbs. sugar snap peas
½ red onion, thinly sliced

1 clove garlic, minced
⅓ c. olive oil

Place peas in a large stockpot and add water to cover; bring to a boil and cook one minute, or until crisp-tender. Drain and rinse; place peas in a large bowl. Add onion, garlic and olive oil; toss gently. Cover and refrigerate at least 20 minutes. Remove from refrigerator and let stand. Serve at room temperature. Serves 8.

Simple Scalloped Tomatoes

This tangy-sweet side is delicious with fish and other seafood.

1 onion, chopped
¼ c. butter
28-oz. can diced tomatoes,
   undrained
5 slices bread, lightly toasted
   and cubed

¼ c. brown sugar, packed
½ t. salt
¼ t. pepper

Cook onion in butter in a skillet over medium-high heat just until tender but not browned. Combine onion mixture and tomatoes in a bowl; add remaining ingredients, and mix well. Pour into a greased 8"x8" baking pan. Bake, uncovered, at 350 degrees for 45 minutes. Serves 4 to 6.

Joan White
Malvern, PA

Marinated Sugar
Snap Peas

Fresh Okra &
Tomato Dish

Fresh Okra + Tomato Dish

A delicious way to enjoy fresh veggies from your garden.

6 slices bacon
3 T. all-purpose flour
4 c. okra, sliced
¾ c. onion, chopped

1 clove garlic, minced
3 c. tomatoes, chopped
½ t. salt
½ t. pepper

In a skillet over medium heat, cook bacon until crisp. Remove bacon and crumble, reserving 3 tablespoons drippings in skillet. Stir flour into drippings. Cook, stirring constantly, until lightly golden. Add okra, onion and garlic. Cook and stir 2 minutes. Stir in tomatoes, salt and pepper. Cover and simmer 15 to 20 minutes, until okra is tender. Sprinkle with crumbled bacon. Serves 6 to 8.

Trudy Satterwhite
San Antonio, TX

Good-For-You Southern Greens

½ c. cooked ham, finely
   chopped
½ c. onion, finely chopped
1 bunch kale, trimmed

½ c. chicken broth
⅛ t. salt
⅛ t. pepper
Garnish: red wine vinegar

In a large skillet over medium heat, cook ham until slightly browned. Add remaining ingredients except vinegar. Cover; simmer 15 minutes, or until kale turns soft and dark. Drizzle with vinegar to taste. Serves 4 to 6.

Aubrey Dunne
Piscataway, NJ

"On a wonderful trip down to North Carolina, our friends took us for authentic eastern North Carolina barbecue. My husband loved the southern collard greens, but not all the fat they were cooked with."

—Aubrey

Mom's Squash Casserole

Loosely cover the casserole with aluminum foil halfway through the baking time so that the crackers don't overbrown.

1½ lbs. zucchini, sliced
1½ lbs. yellow squash, sliced
1 onion, chopped
1 egg, beaten
½ t. salt
¼ t. pepper
½ c. butter, melted and divided
2 c. round buttery crackers, crushed

Cook zucchini and squash in boiling salted water in a large saucepan until tender, about 12 to 15 minutes; drain and mash. Add onion, egg, salt, pepper and half of melted butter. Pour mixture into a greased 13"x9" baking pan. Sprinkle with cracker crumbs; drizzle with remaining butter. Bake, uncovered, at 350 degrees for 30 minutes. Cover and bake an additional 30 minutes. Serves 10 to 12.

Cheryl Donnelly
Arvada, CO

stacking skillets

Protect non-stick skillets from scratching when stacked in a cupboard. . .slip a paper plate or coffee filter in between them.

Garden-Fresh Vegetable Bake

This dish is hearty and filling!

4 yellow squash, coarsely
   chopped
4 zucchini, coarsely chopped
2 T. olive oil
1 bunch green onions, chopped
4 to 5 cloves garlic, minced
10¾-oz. can cream of chicken
   soup

¼ c. milk
8-oz. pkg. cream cheese,
   softened
14¾-oz. can creamed corn
8-oz. pkg. shredded Cheddar
   cheese
salt and pepper to taste
6-oz. pkg. garlic croutons

Combine squash and zucchini in a saucepan; cover with water and simmer over medium-high heat, about 5 minutes. Drain and transfer to a skillet. Stir in olive oil, onions and garlic; sauté over medium heat until tender. Place in a mixing bowl; add soup, milk, cream cheese, corn, cheese, salt and pepper. Mix well; spoon into an ungreased 3-quart casserole dish. Bake, uncovered, at 350 degrees for 35 minutes; sprinkle with croutons. Bake an additional 20 minutes, or until golden and bubbly. Serves 6 to 8.

Michele Hastings
Bedford, TX

Grilled Fresh Veggie Combo

1 zucchini, thinly sliced
1 yellow squash, thinly sliced
1 red onion, thinly sliced
1 T. garlic, minced

olive oil to taste
fresh basil, oregano, rosemary
  or parsley to taste, chopped

Coat inside of a vegetable grill basket with non-stick vegetable spray; fill with vegetables and garlic. Place on a grill preheated to medium heat. Cover and cook until vegetables are crisp-tender. Remove from grill; transfer vegetables to a serving dish. Lightly drizzle with oil; add desired chopped herbs and serve immediately. Serves 6.

Jennifer Weber
Williamsville, NY

"My husband and I created this recipe together when we planted our first garden...we didn't know how to use up all the vegetables we grew! Now we look forward to our fresh veggies every summer."

–Jennifer

Roasted Pepper Potato Topper

With a prep time of only five minutes, this is a must-try recipe. Spooned onto a big baked potato, it's terrific!

8-oz. container sour cream
7-oz. jar roasted red peppers,
  drained and chopped
4 oz. cream cheese, softened

1 clove garlic, minced
1 T. fresh basil, chopped
½ t. dried oregano

Blend together sour cream, red peppers and cream cheese in a bowl. Stir in garlic, basil and oregano until well blended. Chill one hour. Makes about 5 cups.

Jo Ann
Gooseberry Patch

Grilled Fresh
Veggie Combo

Broccoli-Cauliflower Salad

"We grow our own vegetables on our country farm, so I'm always looking for new ways to serve fresh veggies."

—Janice

1 bunch broccoli, chopped
1 head cauliflower, chopped
1 c. green onions, chopped
½ lb. bacon, crisply cooked
  and crumbled
1 c. mayonnaise-type salad
  dressing
½ c. sugar
Garnish: black pepper

Combine broccoli, cauliflower, onions and bacon in a large salad bowl. Mix dressing and sugar in a separate bowl. Drizzle over broccoli mixture; toss together. Serve immediately or cover and refrigerate until serving time. Garnish, if desired. Serves 6 to 8.

Janice Tarter
Morrow, OH

Broccoli Salad of Wonder

3-oz. pkg. ramen noodles, broken up and seasoning packet discarded
1 c. chopped pecans
¼ c. butter, melted
1 bunch broccoli, chopped
12- to 16-oz. pkg. bacon, chopped and crisply cooked
1 head romaine lettuce, finely chopped
1 bunch green onions, chopped

In a bowl, toss uncooked noodles, pecans and melted butter. Spread on an ungreased 15"x10" jelly-roll pan. Bake at 350 degrees for 8 to 10 minutes, until lightly toasted, stirring halfway through. Cool. At serving time, combine noodle mixture with remaining ingredients in a large serving bowl. Drizzle with Dressing; toss to mix. Serves 8 to 10.

Dressing:

1 c. sugar
1 c. olive oil
½ c. red wine vinegar
1 T. soy sauce
salt and pepper to taste

Mix together all ingredients in a bowl; stir until sugar dissolves.

Julia Brasington
Margate, FL

"I first tasted this recipe at a women's Bible study when I was going to Florida State University. The lady who brought it knew that all of us poor, hungry college girls would devour it in seconds. Eight years later, I still make it for special occasions."

–Julia

Browned Butter Mashed Potatoes

Try tossing browned butter with steamed vegetables, or drizzle it over warm, crusty French bread.

¾ c. butter
4 lbs. Yukon Gold potatoes, peeled and cut into 2-inch pieces
1 T. salt
¾ c. buttermilk
½ c. milk
¼ t. pepper
Optional: fresh parsley, rosemary and thyme sprigs

Cook butter in a heavy saucepan over medium heat, stirring constantly, 6 to 8 minutes, just until butter begins to turn golden brown. Immediately remove from heat and pour butter into a small bowl. Remove and reserve one to 2 tablespoons browned butter. Place potatoes in a Dutch oven; cover with water and add salt. Bring to a boil; boil over medium-high heat 20 minutes, or until potatoes are tender. Drain. Reduce heat to low. Return potatoes to Dutch oven; cook, stirring occasionally, 3 to 5 minutes, until potatoes are dry. Mash potatoes with a potato masher to desired consistency. Add remaining ingredients except reserved one to 2 tablespoons butter and fresh herbs; stir just until blended. Transfer to a serving dish. Drizzle with reserved browned butter. Garnish with fresh herbs, if desired. Serves 6 to 8.

tasty veggie plate

Serve up a veggie plate for dinner…a good old southern tradition. With 2 or 3 scrumptious veggie dishes and a basket of buttery cornbread, no one will miss the meat!

Green Chile Rice

Sprinkle with diced jalapeño peppers for an extra kick!

4 c. cooked rice
8-oz. pkg. shredded mozzarella
  cheese

2 c. sour cream
4-oz. can diced green chiles,
  drained

Combine all ingredients in a bowl and mix well. Spoon into an ungreased 2-quart casserole dish. Bake, uncovered, at 400 degrees until bubbly, about 20 minutes. Serves 6.

Debbie Wilson
Weatherford, TX

take-along tips

Prepare the recipe in an ungreased casserole dish and take, unbaked, to your gathering. Bake it just before serving.

Mushroom + Orzo Casserole

An easy-to-make side with flavorful goodness.

8-oz. pkg. orzo pasta, cooked
½ c. margarine, softened
1½-oz. pkg. onion soup mix

8-oz. pkg. sliced mushrooms
¼ c. fresh parsley, chopped

In a bowl, combine orzo, margarine, soup mix and mushrooms. Spoon into an ungreased 2-quart casserole dish; cover and bake at 375 degrees for 30 minutes. Uncover and bake 10 more minutes. Stir in parsley. Serves 6.

Laurie Gross
Thousand Oaks, CA

Spinach Squares

4 c. shredded Cheddar cheese
10-oz. pkg. frozen chopped
   spinach, thawed
1 c. all-purpose flour
2 eggs, beaten

1 c. milk
1 t. salt
1 t. baking powder
½ c. onion, chopped
¼ c. butter, melted

"I find these cheesy squares make a great side or main dish."
—Amy

Blend together all ingredients in a large bowl. Spread in a lightly oiled 13"x9" baking pan. Bake, uncovered, at 350 degrees for 35 minutes. Cool slightly; cut into squares. Makes 9 to 12 servings.

Amy Davila
Fowler, MI

Sweet Potato Casserole

Sweet potatoes with a crunchy golden topping.

40-oz. can sweet potatoes, drained
¾ c. sugar
2 eggs, beaten
⅓ c. evaporated milk
¼ c. butter, melted
1 t. vanilla extract

Mash sweet potatoes in a large bowl; blend in remaining ingredients. Spread in an ungreased 3-quart casserole dish or 8 to 10 ramekins. Spread Topping over sweet potato mixture; bake, uncovered, at 300 degrees for 35 minutes. Serves 8 to 10.

Topping:

⅓ c. butter, melted
1 c. brown sugar, packed
½ c. all-purpose flour
1 c. nuts, chopped

Blend together butter, sugar and flour in a bowl; add chopped nuts and stir.

Jackie Crough
Salina, KS

make-ahead magic

Prepare this casserole a day ahead and store in the refrigerator overnight. Bake casserole before serving.

sweet potato fries

Sweet potato fries are deliciously different! Slice sweet potatoes into strips or wedges, toss with olive oil and place on a baking sheet. Bake at 400 degrees for 20 to 40 minutes, until tender, turning once. Sprinkle with a little cinnamon or sugar for added sweetness or chili powder for a spicy kick.

Three-Bean Basil Salad

Fresh vegetables and basil from your garden will make this wonderful side dish even better!

2 c. canned kidney beans, rinsed

2 c. canned chickpeas, rinsed

2 c. canned green beans, rinsed

1 red onion, sliced and separated into rings

1 carrot, peeled and grated

½ c. vinegar

½ c. vegetable oil

6 T. sugar

1 T. fresh basil, minced

¾ t. dry mustard

salt and pepper to taste

Garnish: fresh basil leaves

Combine beans, onion and carrot in a large bowl. Combine remaining ingredients except garnish in a small bowl and mix well; pour over bean mixture and toss well. Cover and refrigerate overnight; serve chilled. Garnish with basil leaves. Serves 10.

Overnight Oriental Salad

Michelle Allman (Seymour, IN)

¾ c. vegetable oil
½ c. sugar
½ c. white vinegar
2 3-oz. pkgs. Oriental ramen
  noodles with seasoning packets

1 head cabbage, shredded
1 bunch green onions, chopped
1 c. sliced almonds, toasted
1 c. roasted sunflower seeds

Combine oil, sugar, vinegar and seasoning packets from noodles in a bowl and mix well; cover and refrigerate overnight. Crush noodles in a large bowl; add cabbage, green onions, almonds and sunflower seeds. Pour oil mixture over top and toss gently. Serves 10 to 12.

Santa Fe Vegetable Salad

A veggie salad with a sassy dressing!

1 zucchini, diced
½ c. canned corn, drained
5 green onions, chopped
1 red pepper, chopped

1 jicama, peeled and diced
⅓ c. chunky salsa, drained
⅓ c. fresh cilantro, chopped
salt and pepper to taste

Combine all ingredients in a serving bowl; toss with Dressing. Serves 4 to 6.

Dressing:

⅓ c. lime juice
2 t. hot pepper jelly

1 T. water
1 T. olive oil

Mix together all ingredients in a saucepan; heat over medium heat until jelly melts. Stir well.

Laurel Perry
Grayson, GA

Gnocchi + Vegetable Toss

This mixture of tender little potato dumplings and colorful veggies is almost a meal in itself.

17½-oz. pkg. potato gnocchi, uncooked

1 lb. asparagus, cut into bite-size pieces

1 zucchini, halved lengthwise and sliced

1 yellow squash, halved lengthwise and sliced

10-oz. pkg. grape tomatoes, halved

10-oz. jar sun-dried tomato-basil pesto sauce

½ c. sour cream

make-ahead magic

This dish makes great leftovers. Store whatever is left in the refrigerator overnight and serve hot or cold for lunch the next day.

In a stockpot, bring 4 quarts of water to a boil. Add gnocchi and vegetables; return to a boil. Boil 2 to 3 minutes, until gnocchi floats to top; drain. Mix pesto sauce with sour cream in a bowl. Add to gnocchi mixture; toss until thoroughly coated. Serve hot or cold. Makes 4 to 6 servings.

Jennifer Patrick
Delaware, OH

fresh from the market

Farmers' market foods taste so fresh because they're all grown and picked in season at the peak of flavor. . .lettuce, asparagus and strawberries in the springtime, tomatoes, peppers and sweet corn in the summer, and squash and greens in the fall and winter.

Raspberry-Pretzel Salad

1½ c. pretzels, crushed
1 c. sugar, divided
½ c. butter, melted
8-oz. pkg. cream cheese,
  softened
8-oz. container frozen whipped
  topping, thawed

6-oz. pkg. raspberry gelatin mix
2 c. boiling water
2 10-oz. pkgs. frozen
  raspberries

Mix pretzels, ½ cup sugar and butter in a bowl; press into the bottom of an ungreased 13"x9" baking pan to form a crust. Bake at 350 degrees for 5 to 7 minutes; let cool. Combine cream cheese, remaining sugar and whipped topping in a bowl; spread over baked crust and chill. Combine gelatin mix and boiling water in a medium bowl; chill until partially set. Stir in frozen berries; spread over cream cheese layer. Cover and refrigerate until serving time. Makes 12 to 15 servings.

Gean Wilson
Greenwater, WA

"A neighbor shared this recipe with me during a neighborhood barbecue. Now I take this dish along to any barbecue I attend. The next day, people always call me to ask for the recipe."

—Gean

a change of pace

Invite family and friends over for a salad supper. Ask everyone to bring along a favorite salad. You provide crispy bread sticks and a pitcher of iced tea...relax and enjoy!

Strawberry-Melon Salad

"I love to make this dish during strawberry season. It's light yet filling."

—Sandra

1 cantaloupe, peeled and cubed
1 honeydew or Crenshaw melon, peeled and cubed

2 c. strawberries, hulled and quartered

Combine melon cubes in a large bowl. Drizzle with Banana-Yogurt Dressing; toss to mix. Garnish with strawberries and serve immediately. Serves 4.

Banana-Yogurt Dressing:

½ c. plain low-fat yogurt
½ c. orange juice

1 banana, sliced

Combine all ingredients in a blender or food processor. Process ingredients until puréed.

Sandra Bins
Georgetown, TX

Edie's Honeyed Fruit Salad

2 cantaloupes or honeydew melons, peeled and cubed

1 watermelon, peeled and cubed

2 qts. strawberries, hulled and sliced

2 qts. blueberries

1 qt. raspberries

2 lbs. peaches, peeled, pitted and sliced

2 lbs. nectarines, peeled, pitted and sliced

2 lbs. seedless red grapes

1 c. maraschino cherries, drained and halved

honey or sugar to taste

In a very large serving bowl, combine all fruit. Add a little honey or sugar to taste. Toss to mix. Serves 12 to 14.

Edie DeSpain
Logan, UT

"This salad looks so pretty in my large ceramic watermelon bowl. You could also serve it in a carved watermelon half. A refreshing use for ripe fruit!"

—Edie

Summer Corn Salad

"My best friend was hungry for corn salad, so we went to the kitchen to come up with this easy new side! Family-tested and neighbor-approved, it has become a favorite."

–Julie Ann

6 ears sweet corn, kernels
　sliced off
3 tomatoes, chopped
1 green pepper, chopped
1 red onion, chopped
Optional: 1 cucumber, peeled
　and chopped

Optional: 6 green onions,
　chopped
½ c. cider vinegar
⅓ c. olive oil
½ c. sugar
1 t. salt, or more to taste
1 t. pepper, or more to taste

Mix together corn kernels and remaining vegetables in a bowl. In a separate bowl, combine remaining ingredients; whisk until well mixed. Add dressing to vegetables; toss to mix. Cover and refrigerate at least 4 hours before serving. Serves 6.

Julie Ann Perkins
Anderson, IN

Nutty Spinach Salad

Try substituting sweetened dried cranberries for a tangy taste.

10-oz. pkg. baby spinach
2 Granny Smith apples, cored
  and chopped
½ c. cashews
¼ c. golden raisins

¼ c. sugar
¼ c. cider vinegar
¼ c. olive oil
¼ t. garlic salt
¼ t. celery salt

Combine spinach, apples, cashews and raisins in a serving bowl; set aside. Mix remaining ingredients in a jar; cover and shake vigorously. Pour over spinach mixture; toss to coat. Serves 6.

Dilled New Potato Salad

No summer buffet is complete without a big bowl of potato salad. This recipe is extra scrumptious with the fresh flavors of new potatoes, sweet onion and dill. You and your guests will love it!

2 lbs. new potatoes, cut into wedges
10-oz. pkg. frozen petite sweet peas, thawed and drained
½ c. mayonnaise
½ c. plain yogurt

1 sweet onion, chopped
3 T. fresh dill, minced
1 T. Dijon mustard
1 t. garlic salt
¼ t. pepper

In a saucepan, cover potatoes with water. Cook over medium-high heat 20 minutes, or until tender. Drain and add peas. In a large bowl, stir together remaining ingredients. Add potato mixture; toss gently to coat. Cover and chill at least 2 hours. Serves 8.

Linda Stone
Cookeville, TN

fresh...or frozen?

Fresh vegetables are delicous and nutritious if they're used promptly, but don't hesitate to use frozen vegetables instead. Flash-frozen soon after being harvested, frozen veggies retain nutrients and are a real time-saver too. Add them, still frozen, to a simmering pot of soup or a boiling pasta pot.

24-Hour Chopped Salad

A new and different way to serve everyone's favorite seven-layer salad. Add colorful bell peppers too, if you like. You'll want to use your prettiest trifle bowl for this salad!

1 head lettuce, shredded
1 red onion, sliced
1 head cauliflower, cut into
  bite-size pieces
1 c. frozen peas
1 lb. bacon, crisply cooked and
  crumbled

2 c. mayonnaise
⅓ c. grated Parmesan cheese
¼ c. sugar
salt and pepper to taste

take-along tips

Prepare this salad in a serving dish and chill overnight. Wrap tightly with plastic wrap and take to your destination.

Place lettuce in a large serving bowl. Add onion, cauliflower, frozen peas and bacon on top of lettuce. Mix together remaining ingredients in a separate bowl and spread over the top of salad. Cover and refrigerate 24 hours. Toss well before serving. Makes 8 to 10 servings.

Vickie
Gooseberry Patch

Tried & True Apple Casserole

8 to 10 tart apples, peeled,
 cored and halved
½ c. sugar
1 T. all-purpose flour
½ t. cinnamon

¼ t. nutmeg
2 T. butter, diced
Optional: golden raisins,
 chopped walnuts

Place apples in a greased 2-quart casserole dish; set aside. Mix together dry ingredients in a small bowl; sprinkle over apples. Dot with butter. Sprinkle with raisins and walnuts, if desired. Cover and bake at 350 degrees for 45 minutes to one hour. Serves 6 to 8.

Gerry Donnella
Boston, VA

Ginger Ale Baked Apples

A yummy fall dessert or after-the-game snack!

4 baking apples
¼ c. golden raisins, divided
4 t. brown sugar, packed and
 divided

½ c. ginger ale

Core apples but do not cut through bottoms. Place apples in an ungreased 8"x8" baking pan. Spoon one tablespoon raisins and one teaspoon brown sugar into center of each apple. Pour ginger ale over apples. Bake, uncovered, at 350 degrees, basting occasionally with ginger ale, for 45 minutes, or until apples are tender. Serve warm or cold. Serves 4.

Judy Lange
Imperial, PA

Ginger Ale
Baked Apples

Crunchy Fudge,
page 222

blue-ribbon desserts

Everyone knows that dessert is the best part of the meal, so why not start planning your meal here? From cookies to pies to cakes and more, these pages are chock-full of scrumptious sweets. Indulge in Mom's Hummingbird Cake. . .or prepare a favorite like Hello Dolly Bars and cool down on a warm day with Ice Cream Sandwiches.

Grandma's Grange Cookies

"A family favorite that my Grandmother Monnie used to make. Sometimes we like to tint the frosting with food coloring."

—Vivien

⅔ c. butter, softened
1½ c. brown sugar, packed
2 eggs
1 t. vanilla extract
1 t. vinegar

1 c. evaporated milk
2½ to 3 c. all-purpose flour
1 t. baking soda
½ t. baking powder

Blend butter and brown sugar in a bowl; add eggs, vanilla, vinegar and milk. Mix well and set aside. In a separate bowl, sift together flour, baking soda and baking powder; add to butter mixture. Drop by tablespoonfuls onto an ungreased baking sheet; bake at 350 degrees for 10 to 12 minutes, until golden. Cool and spread with Frosting. Makes about 2 dozen.

Frosting:

½ c. butter
¼ c. boiling water

3 c. powdered sugar

Melt butter in a small saucepan; add water and pour over powdered sugar in a mixing bowl. Stir until thick.

Vivien Mullins
Hilliard, OH

sweet tooth satisfaction

Host a "Just Desserts" party. Have friends bring over their favorite sweets. Make sure guests bring a variety of cookies, pies and cakes. Serve it all up with glasses of cold milk or mugs of hot chocolate.

Mom + Me Peanut Butter Kisses

1 c. creamy peanut butter
1 c. sugar
1 egg

24 milk chocolate drops, unwrapped

Combine peanut butter, sugar and egg in a bowl; mix well. Roll into small balls and arrange on an ungreased baking sheet. Bake at 350 degrees for 12 minutes. Remove from oven; immediately place a chocolate drop in the center of each cookie. Makes about 2 dozen.

Nichole Wrigley
Vancouver, WA

"My mom and I first made these for the holidays...but they were so good that we make them year 'round now!"

–Nichole

Chocolate-Butterscotch Cookies

Whip these up in no time. They're perfect with a chilled glass of milk.

1 c. corn syrup
1 c. sugar
1 c. creamy peanut butter
6 c. crispy rice cereal
6-oz. pkg. semi-sweet chocolate chips
6-oz. pkg. butterscotch chips

In a large saucepan, cook corn syrup and sugar over medium heat, stirring frequently, until mixture comes to a boil; remove from heat. Stir in peanut butter and cereal. Press mixture into a greased 13"x9" baking pan. In a double boiler over boiling water, melt chocolate and butterscotch chips over medium heat, stirring constantly, until smooth. Spread mixture over cereal mixture. Refrigerate 15 minutes before cutting into bars. Makes 4 dozen.

Michelle Lamp
Slayton, MN

Cherry Macaroons

1 c. shortening
1 c. sugar
3 eggs
½ c. sour cream
3 c. all-purpose flour
1 t. baking powder
½ t. baking soda
½ t. salt
1 c. shredded coconut
1 t. lemon zest
1½ t. almond extract
⅔ c. candied cherries

Combine shortening, sugar and eggs in a large bowl; mix well and stir in sour cream. Combine flour, baking powder, baking soda and salt in a separate bowl; mix well and add to shortening mixture. Fold in coconut, lemon zest and almond extract. Drop by tablespoonfuls onto ungreased baking sheets. Press one candied cherry onto center of each cookie. Bake at 400 degrees for 10 to 12 minutes. Remove from baking sheets; cool on wire racks. Makes 3½ to 4 dozen.

Cinnamon-Sugar Butter Cookies

2½ c. all-purpose flour
½ t. baking soda
¼ t. salt
1 c. brown sugar, packed
½ c. plus 3 T. sugar, divided

1 c. butter, softened
2 eggs
2 t. vanilla extract
1 T. cinnamon

make-ahead magic
These tasty cookies can be made ahead and frozen for up to one month.

Combine flour, baking soda and salt in a bowl; mix well and set aside. Combine brown sugar and ½ cup sugar in a separate bowl; mix well. Add butter and beat with an electric mixer at medium speed until well blended. Add eggs and vanilla; beat 2 minutes, or until fluffy. Add flour mixture and stir just until blended. Refrigerate dough 30 minutes, or until firm. Shape dough into one-inch balls. Combine remaining 3 tablespoons sugar and cinnamon in a shallow bowl and mix well; roll balls in cinnamon-sugar mixture. Place 2 inches apart on ungreased baking sheets. Bake at 300 degrees for 18 to 20 minutes. Remove from baking sheets; cool on wire racks. Makes 3 dozen.

Caramel-Pecan Bars

16-oz. pkg. yellow cake mix
⅓ c. margarine, softened
2 eggs, divided
14-oz. can sweetened
  condensed milk

1 t. vanilla extract
1 c. chopped pecans
8-oz. pkg. toffee baking bits

Combine cake mix, margarine and one egg in a bowl; mix until crumbly. Pat into a greased 13"x9" baking pan. Combine condensed milk, remaining egg and vanilla in a separate bowl; stir until well blended. Stir in pecans and toffee baking bits. Spread over cake mix mixture. Bake at 350 degrees for 25 to 30 minutes. Cool completely before cutting into bars. Makes one dozen.

Hello Dolly Bars

½ c. margarine, melted
1 c. graham cracker crumbs
1 c. sweetened flaked coconut
6-oz. pkg. semi-sweet
  chocolate chips
6-oz. pkg. butterscotch chips
14-oz. can sweetened
  condensed milk
1 c. chopped pecans

Combine margarine and graham cracker crumbs in a bowl and mix well; press into a lightly greased 9"x9" baking pan. Top with layers of coconut, chocolate chips and butterscotch chips. Pour condensed milk over top; sprinkle with pecans. Bake at 350 degrees for 25 to 30 minutes. Cool; cut into bars. Makes 12 to 16.

Marilyn Morel
Keene, NH

shareable treats

Share leftover bar cookies with friends and neighbors. Package them in cellophane bags tied with colorful ribbons. Include the recipe on a gift tag.

S'mores Brownies
Abi Buening (Grand Forks, ND)

18¼-oz. pkg. brownie mix
3 c. mini marshmallows
4 whole graham crackers, coarsely
  broken

2 1.55-oz. chocolate candy bars,
  broken into small pieces

Prepare and bake brownie mix in a greased 8"x8" baking pan according to package directions. Remove pan from oven and immediately sprinkle brownies with marshmallows and graham cracker pieces. Broil 30 to 60 seconds, until marshmallows are golden, watching carefully because marshmallows brown quickly. Immediately sprinkle with candy bar pieces. Cool 15 minutes before cutting into squares; serve warm. Makes 16.

Lemon Chess Bars

These delicious bars freeze well…keep some on hand to serve to unexpected guests!

½ c. butter or margarine,
  softened
1 c. plus 2 T. all-purpose flour,
  sifted and divided
¼ c. powdered sugar

2 eggs
1 c. sugar
zest of 1 lemon
3 T. lemon juice
additional powdered sugar

Place butter or margarine in a bowl and beat with an electric mixer at medium speed until fluffy. Add one cup flour and ¼ cup powdered sugar and beat well; spoon into an ungreased 8"x8" baking pan and press firmly. Bake at 325 degrees for 20 minutes. Meanwhile, combine eggs, sugar, remaining 2 tablespoons flour, lemon zest and lemon juice in a bowl. Mix well; pour over baked bottom layer. Bake 25 more minutes, or until center is set. Cool. Sprinkle with powdered sugar. Cut into bars. Makes 16.

Caramel-Coffee Tassies

In a word...delicious!

½ c. butter, softened
3-oz. pkg. cream cheese,
   softened
1 c. all-purpose flour

14-oz. pkg. caramels
¼ c. evaporated milk
1½ t. coffee-flavored liqueur
   or brewed coffee

In a bowl, beat together butter and cream cheese until well blended; stir in flour. Form into a ball; cover and chill one hour or overnight. Shape dough into ½-inch balls; press each into an ungreased mini muffin cup. Bake at 350 degrees for 10 to 15 minutes, until golden. Let cool. Combine caramels and evaporated milk in a saucepan over medium heat. Stir frequently until melted. Remove from heat; stir in liqueur or coffee. Spoon caramel filling into baked shells; let cool. Pipe Frosting onto caramel filling. Makes about 2 dozen.

Frosting:

½ c. shortening
⅓ c. sugar
⅓ c. evaporated milk, chilled

½ t. coffee-flavored liqueur
   or brewed coffee

In a bowl, blend shortening and sugar with an electric mixer at medium speed until fluffy; add evaporated milk and liqueur or coffee. Beat at medium-high speed 7 to 10 minutes, until fluffy.

Staci Meyers
Cocoa, FL

Pecan Balls with Fudge Sauce

½ gal. **vanilla ice cream,** softened
2 c. chopped **pecans**

Optional: **frozen whipped topping,** thawed, and **maraschino cherries**

Scoop ice cream into 8 to 10 orange-size balls. Roll in pecans; place in a baking pan, cover and freeze. At serving time, top with Fudge Sauce and, if desired, whipped topping and cherries. Makes 8 to 10 servings.

Fudge Sauce:

½ c. **butter**
2 1-oz. sqs. **unsweetened baking chocolate**

⅔ c. **sugar**
½ c. **evaporated milk**
½ t. **vanilla extract**

Melt butter and chocolate in a saucepan over low heat. Add sugar; stir about 2 to 3 minutes, until smooth. Immediately add evaporated milk and vanilla; mix well and bring to a slow boil. Remove from heat; let cool before pouring over Pecan Balls.

Niki Baltz
Zionsville, IN

"My mother-in-law taught me to make this scrumptious dessert when I was a newlywed."

–Niki

giftable goodie

This delicious Fudge Sauce also makes a great gift. Simply prepare it, let it cool and pour it into a decorative glass jar. Tie on the recipe and give it to friends and neighbors for a perfect present.

Crunchy Fudge

Fudge is always a welcome indulgence...a great gift for friends!

4 c. sugar	6 T. butter
1 c. evaporated milk	1 t. vanilla extract
½ c. corn syrup	

Combine sugar, evaporated milk, corn syrup and butter in a heavy saucepan; heat over medium-low heat until sugar dissolves. Increase heat to medium; heat to boiling, stirring occasionally. Heat, without stirring, to the soft-ball stage, or 234 to 243 degrees on a candy thermometer; remove from heat. Place pan in a 1½-inch deep cold water bath; add vanilla, without stirring. Let cool to 100 degrees; remove from water bath. Blend until fudge thickens and loses its gloss; spread evenly in 2 buttered 8"x8" baking pans. Pour Topping on top; cool. Cut into squares to serve. Makes 3⅓ pounds.

Topping:

1 c. sugar	2 T. evaporated milk
¼ c. water	1 t. vanilla extract
¼ c. butter	1 c. chopped pecans, toasted

Stir together sugar and water in a small skillet; heat over medium-high heat until sugar dissolves. Increase heat to high; stir until mixture turns golden. Remove from heat; carefully add butter, evaporated milk and vanilla, stirring to mix. Add pecans, stirring to coat.

Buckeye Brownies

Chocolate and peanut butter…tastes just like buckeye candies.

19½-oz. pkg. brownie mix
2 c. powdered sugar
½ c. plus 6 T. butter, softened and divided

1 c. creamy peanut butter
6-oz. pkg. semi-sweet chocolate chips

Prepare and bake brownie mix in a greased 13"x9" baking pan according to package directions. Let cool. Mix together powdered sugar, ½ cup butter and peanut butter in a bowl; spread over cooled brownies. Chill one hour. Melt together chocolate chips and remaining butter in a saucepan over low heat, stirring occasionally. Spread over brownies. Let cool; cut into squares. Makes 2 to 3 dozen.

Heather Prentice
Mars, PA

Martha Washingtons

You'll absolutely love this old-fashioned chocolate candy that's chock-full of coconut, nuts and creamy milk…yum!

1 c. butter, melted and cooled
14-oz. can sweetened condensed milk
2 c. powdered sugar
2 c. pecans or walnuts, chopped

14-oz. pkg. sweetened flaked coconut
20-oz. pkg. melting chocolate, chopped

Combine all ingredients except chocolate in a large bowl; mix well and chill overnight. Roll into balls the size of marbles; set on wax paper-lined baking sheets or trays. Microwave chocolate in a microwave-safe bowl on high 1 to 2 minutes, stirring every 30 seconds, until smooth. Dip balls into chocolate and return to wax paper to cool. Makes about 6 dozen.

Renee Velderman
Hopkins, MI

Yummy Chocolate Crunch

So easy to bring along to parties, or even into work.

1 sleeve saltine crackers
1 c. sugar
1 c. butter
12-oz. pkg. chocolate chips

Place crackers, side by side, in a 13"x9" baking pan lined with aluminum foil, until bottom of pan is covered. In a small saucepan, bring sugar and butter to a boil; stir for 3 minutes while boiling. Pour mixture over the crackers and spread with a spatula until all crackers are covered. Bake at 350 degrees for 10 to 15 minutes, until edges of crackers are golden brown. Immediately remove from oven; spread chocolate chips over all until melted. Freeze 2 hours. Break into pieces. Makes 12 to 14 servings.

Rebecca Santelli
Mechanicsville, VA

take-along tips

Transport Yummy Chocolate Crunch to your party in an airtight container. Take along a serving dish.

Blackberry-Apple Crunch

This treat tastes especially delicious after a day of blackberry picking!

2¼ c. all-purpose flour, divided
2½ c. sugar, divided
¼ t. salt
1 c. butter, sliced
2½ c. fresh blackberries
4 lbs. Golden Delicious apples, peeled, cored and thinly sliced
cinnamon to taste
Optional: additional blackberries

Combine 2 cups flour, 1½ cups sugar and salt in a bowl; cut in butter with pastry blender and mix until crumbly. Combine blackberries, apples, remaining ¼ cup flour and remaining sugar in a large bowl; toss to mix and spoon into a greased 13"x9" baking pan. Cover with flour mixture and sprinkle with cinnamon. Bake at 350 degrees for 45 minutes, or until bubbly. Cool slightly before serving. Serve with blackberries, if desired. Serves 12.

Blackberry-Apple
Crunch

Berry Easy Cobbler

Use any favorite fruit…you can't go wrong!

1¼ c. all-purpose flour
½ c. plus ⅓ c. sugar, divided
1½ t. baking powder
¾ c. milk
⅓ c. butter, melted
3 c. blueberries
Garnish: vanilla ice cream or whipped cream

Combine flour, ½ cup sugar and baking powder in a medium mixing bowl. Add milk and butter; stir just until combined. Spread in a greased 8"x8" baking pan. Sprinkle evenly with blueberries, then with remaining sugar. Bake at 350 degrees for 40 to 45 minutes, until a toothpick inserted in the center comes out clean. Serve warm with vanilla ice cream or whipped cream. Makes 4 to 6 servings.

Shelia Taggiano
Castaic, CA

French Apple Crisp

½ c. **butter**, divided
4 c. **apples**, peeled, cored and
  sliced
¼ c. **rum** or **apple juice**
⅔ c. **sugar**, divided
⅛ t. **cinnamon**

½ c. **blanched almonds**,
  finely chopped
½ c. **all-purpose flour**
⅛ t. **salt**
½ t. **vanilla extract**

Melt ¼ cup butter in a large skillet over medium heat. Sauté apples in butter until tender, about 5 minutes. Remove from heat; pour rum or apple juice over apples. Stir in ⅓ cup sugar and cinnamon. Let stand 30 minutes. Measure almonds, flour, remaining sugar and salt into a bowl. Cut in remaining butter with pastry blender or 2 knives until mixture resembles coarse meal. Add vanilla. Evenly spread apple mixture in a greased 2-quart casserole dish or individual ramekins. Sprinkle half of the flour mixture over the apples. Bake at 400 degrees for 15 minutes. Sprinkle remaining flour mixture on top. Bake an additional 15 minutes, or until golden. Serve warm. Serves 10 to 12.

Linda Day
Wall, NJ

"French Apple Crisp is always a favorite because it reminds me of my mother-in-law, who passed the recipe along to me."
—Linda

Grasshopper Pie

If you don't want to use liqueur, add mint extract and a couple of drops of green food coloring.

24 chocolate sandwich
   cookies, crushed and divided
¼ c. margarine, melted
¼ c. crème de menthe liqueur

7½-oz. jar marshmallow
   creme
2 c. whipping cream, whipped

In a medium mixing bowl, combine three-fourths of cookie crumbs and margarine; press into a greased 9" springform pan. In a separate medium mixing bowl, gradually add crème de menthe to marshmallow creme, mixing until well blended. Fold in whipping cream; pour into pan. Sprinkle with remaining crumbs and freeze 2 to 3 hours. Makes 8 servings.

Caryn Dubelko
Dayton, OH

Fudge-Brownie Pie

"This recipe first appeared in a 1914 cookbook published by the YMCA, and it's as good now as it was then."

—Flo

1 c. sugar
½ c. margarine, melted
2 eggs
½ c. all-purpose flour

⅓ c. baking cocoa
¼ t. salt
1 t. vanilla extract
½ c. chopped pecans

In a mixing bowl, beat sugar and margarine. Add eggs; mix well. Stir in flour, cocoa and salt; mix in vanilla and pecans. Pour into a greased and floured 9" pie plate; bake at 350 degrees for 25 to 30 minutes. Serves 6.

Flo Burtnett
Gage, OK

Old Dominion Chess Pie

Carol Hickman (Kingsport, TN)

Think of it as chocolate pecan pie…yum!

9-inch refrigerated pie crust
5 T. baking cocoa
1½ c. sugar
2 eggs, beaten
½ c. chopped pecans

¼ c. butter, melted
½ c. evaporated milk
½ c. flaked coconut
Garnish: whipped cream

Fit pie crust into a 9" pie plate; crimp. In a large bowl, mix together all remaining ingredients except garnish; pour into pie crust. Bake at 400 degrees for 30 minutes. Let cool completely. Garnish with whipped cream. Serves 6 to 8.

Crustless Coconut Pie

The ultimate dessert when you discover you don't have a pie crust on hand!

4 eggs
1¾ c. sugar
2 c. milk
¼ c. butter, melted
½ c. self-rising flour

1 c. flaked coconut
1 t. vanilla extract
Optional: whipped cream,
   toasted flaked coconut

In a large bowl, beat eggs until frothy. Add remaining ingredients except garnish in order given; mix well. Spread in 2 ungreased 9" pie plates; bake at 350 degrees for 25 to 30 minutes, until golden. Garnish with whipped cream and toasted coconut, if desired. Makes 2 pies, 6 to 8 servings each.

Glenda Geohagen
DeFuniak Springs, FL

Peanut Butter Strudel Pie

The best peanut butter pie! Topped with meringue, it's wonderful.

¾ c. powdered sugar
¼ c. creamy peanut butter
9-inch refrigerated pie crust, baked
⅔ c. plus 6 T. sugar, divided
⅓ c. all-purpose flour

¼ t. salt
2 c. milk
3 eggs, separated
2 T. butter
½ t. vanilla extract
¼ t. cream of tartar

In a small bowl, combine powdered sugar and peanut butter to resemble coarse crumbs. Spread over bottom of pie crust, reserving one tablespoon for topping. In a 2-quart saucepan, stir together ⅔ cup sugar, flour and salt; gradually add milk. Bring mixture to a boil over medium heat, stirring constantly; cook and stir 5 minutes or until thickened. Remove from heat and set aside. In a small bowl, beat egg yolks and blend in a small amount of milk mixture; stir well. Return egg mixture to hot mixture in pan; cook and stir over low heat 3 minutes. Remove from heat and stir in butter and vanilla. Cover and set filling aside. In a medium bowl, beat egg whites and cream of tartar until foamy. Gradually beat in remaining sugar, one tablespoon at a time, beating until stiff peaks form. Reheat filling over medium heat, stirring constantly, just until hot. Pour hot filling over peanut butter crumbs in pie crust. Spread meringue over pie, being sure to touch edges of crust to seal. Sprinkle reserved peanut butter crumbs over meringue. Bake at 325 degrees for 25 minutes, or until meringue is golden. Cool completely before serving. Serves 6 to 8.

Phyllis Laughrey
Mt. Vernon, OH

make-ahead magic

Prepare the pie in advance without baking and store overnight in the refrigerator. Bake before serving.

Fruit Compote

Most any summer fruit will do. Here's our recipe...

Syrup:
1 c. water
½ c. sugar
¾ c. fresh mint, chopped
¼ c. bourbon
1 T. fresh lemon juice

Compote:
¼ cantaloupe, seeded
¼ honeydew melon, seeded
½ lb. sweet cherries, pitted
3 ripe peaches, thinly sliced
3 T. fresh mint, thinly sliced
Garnish: fresh mint sprigs

To make syrup, combine water and sugar in a medium saucepan over low heat until sugar dissolves. Add mint and boil 5 minutes over medium heat. Let cool completely. Strain into a bowl, pressing firmly on the mint to extract flavor. Mix bourbon and lemon juice into syrup. Cover and refrigerate; the syrup can be made ahead of time. Scoop melons with a melon baller. Combine all fruits in a large bowl; add syrup and toss. Refrigerate 30 minutes. Spoon into pretty pedestal glasses and garnish with mint sprigs. Makes 4 servings.

Mississippi Dirt Pudding

Kids and adults alike are amused by this pudding! Just for fun, make it in a clean new flowerpot, poke in a plastic flower and serve with a trowel.

¼ c. butter, softened
8-oz. pkg. cream cheese, softened
1 c. powdered sugar
3½ c. milk
2 5¼-oz. pkgs. instant vanilla pudding mix

12-oz. container frozen whipped topping, thawed
20-oz. pkg. chocolate sandwich cookies, crushed and divided
Optional: gummy worms

Combine butter and cream cheese in a large bowl; mix until creamy. Stir in powdered sugar, milk and pudding mix; beat well. Fold in whipped topping. Layer one-third of the cookie crumbs in the bottom of an ungreased 13"x9" baking pan or 8 to 10 individual bowls or pots. Top with half of the pudding mixture, another layer of crumbs, the remaining pudding and the remaining crumbs. Cover and refrigerate 2 hours to overnight. Garnish with gummy worms, if desired. Makes 8 to 10 servings.

Rob McKelvy
Roswell, NM

dirt pudding to go

You can also prepare this pudding in clear plastic cups and serve with plastic spoons. It makes a fun treat for a class party or neighborhood block party.

Creamy Raspberry Mousse

It's a snap to make this elegant dessert.

1½ c. white chocolate chips
1 c. milk
12-oz. pkg. frozen raspberries, thawed
2 to 3 T. sugar
2 3.9-oz. pkgs. white chocolate instant pudding mix
2 c. frozen whipped topping, thawed
Optional: ½ c. chopped pistachios

Combine white chocolate chips and milk in a large microwave-safe bowl. Microwave on high 15 seconds at a time, stirring between each interval, until chips are melted. Place in refrigerator until cold; stir occasionally to minimize separation. Process raspberries and sugar in a blender until smooth. Strain seeds, if desired; set aside. When chocolate mixture is cold, add pudding mix; beat with an electric mixer at medium speed about 2 minutes. Fold in whipped topping; refrigerate at least one hour. Divide among 6 individual serving bowls; top each with about 2 tablespoons of raspberry mixture. Sprinkle with pistachios, if desired. Makes 6 servings.

Marcia Marcoux
Charlton, MA

get crafty

Invite friends over for an arts and crafts night. Provide materials to decorate holiday items such as pumpkins, ornaments or Valentine cards. Serve a delicious dessert and let the fun begin!

Cookies + Cream Dessert

Cookies, pudding and whipped topping...no one can resist this!

14.5-oz. pkg. chocolate
sandwich cookies, crushed
½ c. butter, melted
2 3.4-oz. pkgs. instant vanilla
pudding mix
3 c. milk

8-oz. pkg. cream cheese,
softened
8-oz. container frozen
whipped topping, thawed
Optional: 8 chocolate
sandwich cookies, halved

make-ahead magic

Prepare this dessert a day ahead and store in the refrigerator overnight. Remove from refrigerator and garnish just before serving.

Mix cookie crumbs with butter in a medium bowl; reserve one cup of mixture. Press remaining mixture in the bottom of an ungreased 13"x9" baking pan or individual serving dishes; set aside. In a large bowl, combine pudding mix, milk, cream cheese and whipped topping; spread over cookie crumb mixture. Sprinkle with reserved cookie crumb mixture; refrigerate one hour. Garnish with cookie halves, if desired. Serves 15.

Jodi Wieland
Templeton, IA

Blue-Ribbon Banana Cake

½ c. shortening
¼ c. plus 2 T. butter, softened and divided
2 c. sugar, divided
2 eggs
1 c. banana, mashed
1 c. chopped pecans, divided
2 c. cake flour
1 t. baking soda
1 t. baking powder
¾ t. salt, divided
2 t. vanilla extract, divided
½ c. buttermilk
¼ c. sweetened flaked coconut
½ c. all-purpose flour
½ c. half-and-half
Garnish: sweetened flaked coconut

Combine shortening, ¼ cup butter and 1½ cups sugar in a large bowl; beat with an electric mixer at medium speed until fluffy. Add eggs and banana; beat 2 minutes. Stir in ½ cup pecans. In a medium bowl, sift together cake flour, baking soda, baking powder and ½ teaspoon salt; add to shortening mixture. Add one teaspoon vanilla and buttermilk; beat 2 minutes. Divide batter equally between 2 greased and floured 9" round cake pans; sprinkle batter with coconut. Bake at 350 degrees for 25 to 30 minutes. Cool cakes 10 minutes before removing from pans. Combine remaining ½ cup sugar, all-purpose flour, half-and-half and remaining 2 tablespoons butter in a saucepan over medium heat; cook until thickened, whisking frequently. Add remaining ½ cup nuts, ¼ teaspoon salt and one teaspoon vanilla, stirring well; cool. Place first cake layer, coconut-side down, on a serving platter; spread thickened sugar mixture over top. Place second layer, coconut-side up, over first layer. Swirl on Snow White Frosting, leaving center of cake unfrosted so coconut can be seen. Garnish with additional sweetened flaked coconut. Serves 12 to 16.

Snow White Frosting:

1 egg white
¼ c. shortening
¼ c. butter, softened
½ t. vanilla extract
¼ t. almond extract
2 c. powdered sugar

Combine egg white, shortening, butter and extracts in a large bowl; blend well. Gradually add powdered sugar, beating until fluffy.

Cora's Jam Cake

2½ c. all-purpose flour
⅔ c. butter, melted
1 c. seedless blackberry jam
⅔ c. sour cream
2 eggs, beaten
1 c. sugar
1 t. baking soda

1 t. ground cloves
1 t. cinnamon
1 t. allspice
1 t. nutmeg
Garnish: fresh blackberries,
   thyme sprigs

Combine all ingredients except garnish in a large bowl; mix well. Pour into a greased and floured 13"x9" baking pan. Bake at 350 degrees for 25 minutes, or until toothpick inserted in center of cake comes out clean. Cool; spread with Caramel Frosting. Garnish with blackberries and thyme sprigs. Serves 8.

Caramel Frosting:

½ c. butter
1 c. brown sugar, packed

¼ c. milk
2 c. powdered sugar

Melt butter in a saucepan. Add brown sugar and milk; cook over low heat. Gradually add powdered sugar, beating well after each addition, until thick enough to spread.

Carma Brown
Xenia, OH

"My grandmother had this recipe written down in a notebook dated 1941."

—Carma

Old-Fashioned Shortcake

Strawberry shortcake is traditional, but other ripe, juicy fruits like peaches and blueberries make tasty shortcake too!

4 c. all-purpose flour
¼ c. sugar
2 T. plus 2 t. baking powder
1 t. salt

6 T. shortening
1½ c. milk
Garnish: butter, strawberries, whipped cream

Sift together dry ingredients in a mixing bowl; add shortening and enough milk to make a soft dough. Spread in a greased 13"x9" baking pan. Bake at 350 degrees for 20 to 25 minutes, until golden. Cool; cut into squares. To serve, split open each square; spread bottom halves lightly with butter. Top with strawberries and whipped cream; add top halves. Makes 8 to 10 servings.

Nancy Molldrem
Eau Claire, WI

pick your own

Many strawberry farms now allow you to pick your own strawberries. Try finding such a farm in your area. Most also serve up delicious homemade treats, such as strawberry ice cream and preserves.

Mom's Hummingbird Cake

3 c. all-purpose flour
2 c. sugar
1 t. baking soda
1 t. cinnamon
½ t. salt
3 eggs, beaten

¾ c. oil
1½ t. vanilla extract
8-oz. can crushed pineapple
1¾ c. bananas, mashed
1½ c. chopped pecans, divided

In a large bowl, combine flour, sugar, baking soda, cinnamon and salt. Add eggs and oil; stir just until dry ingredients are moistened. Stir in vanilla, pineapple, bananas and one cup pecans. Pour into 3 greased and floured 9" round cake pans. Bake at 350 degrees for 25 to 30 minutes. Cool in pans 10 minutes; remove from pans and let cool completely. Spread Cream Cheese Frosting between layers and on top and sides of cake. Sprinkle remaining pecans on top. Makes 8 to 10 servings.

Cream Cheese Frosting:

1 c. margarine, softened
2 8-oz. pkgs. cream cheese, softened

2 16-oz. pkgs. powdered sugar
2 t. vanilla extract

In a large bowl, blend together margarine and cream cheese. Gradually add powdered sugar; beat until mixture is light and fluffy. Stir in vanilla.

Laurie Wilson
Fort Wayne, IN

"My mom used to make this scrumptious cake for me...its flavor is outstanding. Thanks for the memories, Mom!"

–Laurie

Granny's Apple
Coffee Cake

Granny's Apple Coffee Cake

1½ c. all-purpose flour
¾ c. sugar
2 t. baking powder
1 t. cinnamon
¼ t. salt

½ c. butter, softened
2 eggs
¾ c. milk
2¼ c. apples, peeled, cored, sliced and divided

Combine flour, sugar, baking powder, cinnamon and salt in a bowl; mix well. Blend in butter, eggs and milk; pour half of batter into a greased and floured 9"x9" baking pan. Arrange half of apples over batter; sprinkle with half of the Topping. Arrange remaining apples over Topping, followed by remaining batter and remaining Topping. Bake at 350 degrees for 40 minutes. Makes 16 servings.

Topping:

½ c. brown sugar, packed
3 T. all-purpose flour
½ c. chopped walnuts

1½ t. cinnamon
1 T. butter

Combine all ingredients in a bowl; mix well.

Phyllis Cowgill
La Porte, IN

"I remember my mother and great-grandmother making this cake with apples and butternuts picked right off the tree and fresh milk from our cows. It's good on a cold brisk morning with a cup of coffee."

—Phyllis

Granny Pursley's Pound Cake

2 c. sugar
1 c. olive oil
2 c. all-purpose flour

5 T. milk
1 T. vanilla extract
5 eggs

Combine all ingredients in a mixing bowl, beating in eggs one at a time. Pour into a greased 10" Bundt® pan. Bake at 350 degrees for 30 minutes; reduce oven temperature to 325 degrees and bake an additional 30 minutes. Serves 8 to 10.

Sandra Pursley
Ooltewah, TN

"Granny always made this cake for church dinners."

—Sandra

Charlotte's Chocolate Sheet Cake

"My mother-in-law is famous for this cake in our family... all 22 grandchildren request it when we get together."

—Terri

1 c. margarine
1 c. water
¼ c. baking cocoa
2 c. all-purpose flour
2 c. sugar

1 t. baking soda
⅛ t. salt
½ c. buttermilk
2 eggs, beaten

Place margarine, water and cocoa in a saucepan. Heat until margarine melts; let cool. In a mixing bowl, combine flour, sugar, baking soda and salt; mix well. Add margarine mixture, buttermilk and eggs to flour mixture; stir well. Spread in a greased 15"x10" jelly-roll pan. Bake at 400 degrees for 20 minutes. Serves 15 to 20.

Terri Lock
Waverly, MO

the right timing...

To avoid overcooking, set your timer for 3 minutes fewer than the allotted time. Ovens can vary in temperature, so checking for doneness a little early will ensure excellent baked goods every time.

Chocolate-Peanut Butter Cupcakes

1 T. whipping cream, heated
2 oz. semi-sweet baking
   chocolate, grated
⅔ c. plus 2 t. sugar, divided
¼ c. creamy peanut butter
6 oz. semi-sweet baking
   chocolate

6 T. butter
2 eggs
1 t. vanilla extract
¾ c. all-purpose flour
¼ t. baking soda
¼ t. salt
16-oz. container white frosting

Pour hot whipping cream over 2 ounces grated chocolate and 2 tea-spoons sugar in a bowl; stir until combined and chocolate melts. Add peanut butter and mix well; refrigerate 35 to 40 minutes, until slightly firm. Combine 6 ounces chocolate and butter in the top of a double boiler over boiling water; cook over low heat until butter and chocolate melt. Place eggs in a large bowl and beat with an electric mixer at medium speed until foamy; add remaining ⅔ cup sugar and vanilla and beat until fluffy. Add melted chocolate mixture and beat at low speed until mixed. Add flour, baking soda and salt and beat just until combined. Pour batter into lightly greased muffin cups, filling almost two-thirds full. Roll rounded teaspoonfuls of filling into balls and press one ball lightly into the center of each cupcake. Bake at 350 degrees for 15 to 20 minutes. Cool completely before frosting. Makes one dozen.

Ice Cream Sandwiches

Keep these in your freezer for those hot summer days when the kids want a treat!

take-along tips

Transport these treats to your gathering in a cooler. Either serve immediately or store in the freezer until ready to serve.

3.4-oz. pkg. instant vanilla pudding mix
2 c. milk
2 c. frozen whipped topping, thawed
1 c. semi-sweet mini chocolate chips
24 graham crackers, halved

Mix pudding and milk in a bowl according to package directions; refrigerate until set. Fold in whipped topping and chocolate chips. Arrange 24 graham cracker halves on a baking sheet; top each with about 3 tablespoons of filling. Top each with another graham cracker half. Wrap individually in plastic wrap. Freeze one hour or until firm. Makes 2 dozen.

Shari Miller
Hobart, IN

cookie swap

You can make festive ice cream sandwiches using a variety of cookies, such as cookies from the bakery, large shortbread cookies or with your favorite chocolate chip cookie recipe.

Chocolate-Cappuccino Cheesecake

This makes an absolutely delicious gift…if you can bear to give it away!

1½ c. pecans, finely chopped
1½ c. chocolate wafer cookies, crushed
⅓ c. butter, melted
½ c. semi-sweet chocolate chips, melted

Combine pecans, cookies and butter in a medium bowl; press into bottom and up sides of a greased 9" springform pan. Drizzle with chocolate; chill until chocolate is firm. Pour Filling into crust; bake at 300 degrees for one hour and 10 minutes. Cool completely. Cover and chill 8 hours. Spread Topping over cake. Remove sides of pan. Serves 12.

Filling:

2 8-oz. pkgs. cream cheese, softened
1½ c. semi-sweet chocolate chips, melted and cooled
1 c. brown sugar, packed
4 eggs, beaten
1 c. sour cream
⅓ c. cold coffee
2 t. vanilla extract

Combine all ingredients in a large bowl; blend until smooth.

Topping:

⅔ c. whipping cream
¼ c. sugar
½ c. semi-sweet chocolate chips

In a saucepan, heat whipping cream and sugar over low heat, whisking constantly. Add chocolate chips, whisking until smooth.

Sandy Stacy
Medway, OH

make-ahead magic

This decadent cheesecake can be made a day ahead and stored overnight in the refrigerator.

METRIC EQUIVALENTS

The recipes that appear in this cookbook use the standard U.S. method for measuring liquid and dry or solid ingredients (teaspoons, tablespoons and cups). The information in the following charts is provided to help cooks outside the United States successfully use these recipes. All equivalents are approximate.

METRIC EQUIVALENTS FOR DIFFERENT TYPES OF INGREDIENTS

A standard cup measure of a dry or solid ingredient will vary in weight depending on the type of ingredient.
A standard cup of liquid is the same volume for any type of liquid.
Use the following chart when converting standard cup measures to grams (weight) or milliliters (volume).

Standard Cup	Fine Powder (ex. flour)	Grain (ex. rice)	Granular (ex. sugar)	Liquid Solids (ex. butter)	Liquid (ex. milk)
1	140 g	150 g	190 g	200 g	240 ml
¾	105 g	113 g	143 g	150 g	180 ml
⅔	93 g	100 g	125 g	133 g	160 ml
½	70 g	75 g	95 g	100 g	120 ml
⅓	47 g	50 g	63 g	67 g	80 ml
¼	35 g	38 g	48 g	50 g	60 ml
⅛	18 g	19 g	24 g	25 g	30 ml

USEFUL EQUIVALENTS FOR LIQUID INGREDIENTS BY VOLUME

¼ tsp =				1 ml
½ tsp =				2 ml
1 tsp =				5 ml
3 tsp = 1 Tbsp		= ½ fl oz	=	15 ml
2 Tbsp	= ⅛ c	= 1 fl oz	=	30 ml
4 Tbsp	= ¼ c	= 2 fl oz	=	60 ml
5⅓ Tbsp	= ⅓ c	= 3 fl oz	=	80 ml
8 Tbsp	= ½ c	= 4 fl oz	=	120 ml
10⅔ Tbsp	= ⅔ c	= 5 fl oz	=	160 ml
12 Tbsp	= ¾ c	= 6 fl oz	=	180 ml
16 Tbsp	= 1 c	= 8 fl oz	=	240 ml
1 pt	= 2 c	= 16 fl oz	=	480 ml
1 qt	= 4 c	= 32 fl oz	=	960 ml
		33 fl oz	=	1000 ml = 1 liter

USEFUL EQUIVALENTS FOR DRY INGREDIENTS BY WEIGHT

(To convert ounces to grams, multiply the number of ounces by 30.)

1 oz	=	¹⁄₁₆ lb	=	30 g
4 oz	=	¼ lb	=	120 g
8 oz	=	½ lb	=	240 g
12 oz	=	¾ lb	=	360 g
16 oz	=	1 lb	=	480 g

USEFUL EQUIVALENTS FOR LENGTH

(To convert inches to centimeters, multiply the number of inches by 2.5.)

1 in		= 2.5 cm	
6 in = ½ ft		= 15 cm	
12 in = 1 ft		= 30 cm	
36 in = 3 ft = 1 yd		= 90 cm	
40 in		= 100 cm	= 1 meter

USEFUL EQUIVALENTS FOR COOKING/OVEN TEMPERATURES

	Fahrenheit	Celsius	Gas Mark
Freeze Water	32° F	0° C	
Room Temperature	68° F	20° C	
Boil Water	212° F	100° C	
Bake	325° F	160° C	3
	350° F	180° C	4
	375° F	190° C	5
	400° F	200° C	6
	425° F	220° C	7
	450° F	230° C	8
Broil			Grill

index

sandwiches

sides

salsas and sauces

soups & stews

Everyday One-Dish Meals

ISBN-13: 978-0-8487-0118-5
ISBN-10: 0-8487-0118-6

Library of Congress Control Number: 2014930619
Printed in the United States of America
First Printing 2014

Oxmoor House

Vice President, Brand Publishing: Laura Sappington
Editorial Director: Leah McLaughlin
Creative Director: Felicity Keane
Brand Manager: Vanessa Tiongson
Senior Editor: Rebecca Brennan
Managing Editor: Elizabeth Tyler Austin
Assisant Managing Editor: Jeanne de Lathouder

Gooseberry Patch Everyday One-Dish Meals

Editor: Susan Ray
Art Director: Christopher Rhoads
Assistant Designer: Allison Sperando Potter
Executive Food Director: Grace Parisi
Assistant Test Kitchen Manager: Alyson Moreland Haynes
Recipe Developers and Testers: Wendy Ball, R.D.; Tamara Goldis; Stefanie Maloney; Callie Nash; Karen Rankin; Leah Van Deren
Food Stylists: Victoria E. Cox; Margaret Monroe Dickey, Catherine Crowell Steele
Photography Director: Jim Bathie
Senior Photographer: Hélène Dujardin
Senior Photo Stylist: Kay E. Clarke
Photo Stylist: Mindi Shapiro Levine
Assistant Photo Stylist: Mary Louise Menendez
Production Manager: Theresa Beste-Farley
Associate Production Manager: Amy Mangus

Contributors

Project Editor: Laura Medlin
Copy Editors: Lucia Carruthers, Jasmine Hodges
Proofreader: Adrienne Davis
Interns: Ali Carruba, Frances Higginbotham, Elizabeth Laseter, Amy Pinney, Madison Taylor Pozzo, Deanna Sakal, April Smitherman, Megan Thompson, Tonya West
Food Stylist: Ashley Strickland Freeman
Photographer: Mary Britton Senseney
Photo Stylist: Elizabeth Demos

Time Home Entertainment Inc.

Publisher: Jim Childs
Vice President, Brand & Digital Strategy: Steven Sandonato
Vice President, Finance: Vandana Patel
Executive Director, Marketing Services: Carol Pittard
Executive Director, Retail & Special Sales: Tom Mifsud
Executive Publishing Director: Joy Butts
Associate Publishing Director: Megan Pearlman
Director, Bookazine Development & Marketing: Laura Adam
Associate General Counsel: Helen Wan

To order additional publications,
call 1-800-765-6400 or 1-800-491-0551.

For more books to enrich your life, visit **oxmoorhouse.com**

To search, savor, and share thousands of recipes,
visit **myrecipes.com**

Front Cover (from left to right, top to bottom):
Grilled Salmon BLTs (page 161), Momma's Divine Divan (page 63), Deep-Dish Skillet Pizza (page 141)

Page 1: Cream Cheese Enchiladas (page 45)

Back Cover (from left to right, top to bottom): Easy Southern-Style Pork Barbecue (page 109), Mom's Hummingbird Cake (page 241), Pasta with Roasted Veggies (page 169)

Our Story

Back in 1984, we were next-door neighbors raising our families in the little town of Delaware, Ohio. Two moms with small children, we were looking for a way to do what we loved and stay home with the kids too. We had always shared a love of home cooking and making memories with family & friends and so, after many a conversation over the backyard fence, **Gooseberry Patch** was born.

We put together our first catalog at our kitchen tables, enlisting the help of our loved ones wherever we could. From that very first mailing, we found an immediate connection with many of our customers, and it wasn't long before we began receiving letters, photos and recipes from these new friends. In 1992, we put together our very first cookbook, compiled from hundreds of these recipes, and the rest, as they say, is history.

Hard to believe it's been over 25 years since those kitchen-table days! From that original little **Gooseberry Patch** family, we've grown to include an amazing group of creative folks who love cooking, decorating and creating as much as we do. Today, we're best known for our homestyle, family-friendly cookbooks, now recognized as national bestsellers.

One thing's for sure, we couldn't have done it without our friends all across the country. Each year, we're honored to turn thousands of your recipes into our collectible cookbooks. Our hope is that each book captures the stories and heart of all of you who have shared with us. Whether you've been with us since the beginning or are just discovering us, welcome to the **Gooseberry Patch** family!

We couldn't make our best-selling cookbooks without YOU!

Each of our books is filled with recipes from cooks just like you, gathered from kitchens all across the country.

Share your tried & true recipes with us on our website and you could be selected for an upcoming cookbook. If your recipe is included, you'll receive a FREE copy of the cookbook when it's published!

www.gooseberrypatch.com

We'd love to add YOU to our Circle of Friends!

Get free recipes, crafts, giveaways and so much more when you join our email club...join us online at all the spots below for even more goodies!